lonely planet

Diving & Snorkeling

New Zealand

Jenny & Tony Enderby

LONELY PLANET PUBLICATIONS
Melbourne • Oakland • London • Paris

Diving & Snorkeling New Zealand
- A Lonely Planet Pisces Book

1st Edition – October 2002

Published by
Lonely Planet Publications Pty Ltd, ABN 36 005 607 983
90 Maribyrnong St., Footscray, Victoria 3011, Australia

Other offices
150 Linden Street, Oakland, California 94607, USA
10a Spring Place, London NW5 3BH, UK
1 rue du Dahomey, 75011 Paris, France

Photographs
by Jenny & Tony Enderby (unless otherwise noted)

Front cover photograph
Rainbow Warrior, by Darryl Torckler

Back cover photographs
Bottlenose dolphins in the Hauraki Gulf
Jason mirabilis nudibranch on colorful wall
Waterfalls in Milford Sound, Fiordland

Most of the images in this guide are available for
licensing from **Lonely Planet Images**
www.lonelyplanetimages.com

ISBN 1 74059 267 0

text & maps © Lonely Planet Publications Pty Ltd 2002
photographs © photographers as indicated 2002
dive site maps are Transverse Mercator projection

Printed by H&Y Printing Ltd., Hong Kong

Contents

Authors

Jenny & Tony Enderby

Jenny and Tony are internationally published photo-journalists who specialize in natural history, travel and adventure. They started taking underwater photographs in 1991 and have since won many photographic awards in New Zealand and overseas. They've taken photographs for three NZ marine life identification guides and are the authors/photographers of an illustrated book about Goat Island Marine Reserve, where they teach visitors about resident marine life. Jenny and Tony live in Leigh, north of Auckland. Find them on the internet at www.enderby.co.nz.

From the Authors

We'd like to thank the divers and diving services throughout New Zealand who helped with information, boat trips and Kiwi hospitality. Special thanks to Dave Moran of *Dive New Zealand* for helping to sow the seed that started the project. Thanks also to: Carol and Jackie Green; Murray and Joanne Long; Kay and Justin Calder; Julie and Mason Stretch; Laurie and Rosemary Petherick; Katrina and Grant Hunter; Wendy and Ian Moffat; Marcel and Helena de Ruiter of EIC Ltd.; Russ Cochrane and Wendy Helms of Cathedral Cove Dive & Snorkel; Maria and Floor Anthoni of Seafriends; Sarah Stirrup and Dave Johnson of Tawaki Dive; Brent McFadden of NZ Sea Adventures; Peter and Iris Tait aboard *Talisker*; David and Jayne Valli of Oban Tours; Dennis and Lynette Buurman of Dolphin Encounter, Kaikoura; Vic and Fizz Foster of Shark Dive Kaikoura; Submarine Adventures; Bob Begg, Dave Watson and staff at Dive Otago; Dive HQ Tauranga; Tauranga Underwater Centre; Tony and Louise Bonne of Whakatane PADI Dive Centre; Rob and Lyn Phillips of Black Shag Charters; Juroen Jongejans and Glenn Edney of Dive! Tutukaka; Frank Carre of Sandpiper Charters; and Roslyn Bullas and David Lauterborn of Lonely Planet Publications.

Photography Notes

Underwater, Jenny and Tony use Pentax SFX, SF1 and Z-1P cameras in Ikelite housings with Ikelite AI, AIN and MV strobes and a Sea & Sea YS-30 slave strobe. For macro and close-up photography they prefer either a 50mm lens or a 105mm macro lens. For wide-angle photography they use a 20mm lens. Topside, they work with the Pentax cameras and a variety of lenses. They use Fujichrome Velvia film.

Contributing Photographers

Jenny and Tony Enderby took most of the photographs in this book. Thanks also to Laurence Belcher, Roslyn Bullas and Darryl Torckler (www.darryltorckler.com).

From the Publisher

This first edition was published in Lonely Planet's U.S. office under the guidance of Roslyn Bullas, the Pisces Books publishing manager. David Lauterborn edited the text and photos with buddy checks from Roslyn Bullas. Emily Douglas designed the cover and the book's interior. Justin Marler illustrated the *Mikhail Lermontov*. Navigating the nautical charts was cartographer Brad Lodge, who created the maps, with assistance from Graham Neale and Justin Colgan. U.S. cartography manager Alex Guilbert supervised map production. Lindsay Brown reviewed the Marine Life section for scientific accuracy. Portions of the text were adapted from Lonely Planet's *New Zealand*.

Pisces Pre-Dive Safety Guidelines

Before embarking on a scuba diving, skin diving or snorkeling trip, carefully consider the following to help ensure a safe and enjoyable experience:

- Possess a current diving certification card from a recognized scuba diving instructional agency (if scuba diving)
- Be sure you are healthy and feel comfortable diving
- Obtain reliable information about physical and environmental conditions at the dive site (e.g., from a reputable local dive operation)
- Be aware of local laws, regulations and etiquette about marine life and environment
- Dive at sites within your experience level; if possible, engage the services of a competent, professionally trained dive instructor or divemaster

Underwater conditions vary significantly from one region, or even site, to another. Seasonal changes can significantly alter site and dive conditions. These differences influence the way divers dress for a dive and what diving techniques they use.

There are special requirements for diving in any area, regardless of location. Before your dive, ask about environmental characteristics that can affect your diving and how trained local divers deal with these considerations.

Warning & Request

Things change—dive site conditions, regulations, topside information. Nothing stays the same for long. Your feedback on this book will be used to help update and improve the next edition. Excerpts from your correspondence may appear in *Planet Talk*, our quarterly newsletter, or *Comet*, our monthly email newsletter. Please let us know if you do not want your letter published or your name acknowledged.

Correspondence can be addressed to:
Lonely Planet Publications
Pisces Books
150 Linden Street
Oakland, CA 94607
email: pisces@lonelyplanet.com

Introduction

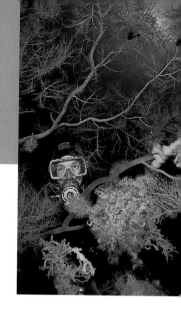

Though small in landmass, New Zealand is richly endowed with magnificent scenery and a variety of outdoor attractions and activities. Virgin bushland, mighty mountain ranges, ancient forests, bubbling thermal pools, and icy glaciers and fiords are but some of its compelling natural features. Then there's the water: The country's serpentine coastline is almost as long as that of the continental United States.

No New Zealander lives more than an hour or two by car from the sea, so watersports naturally play a prominent role. In fact, 10% of New Zealanders have completed a basic scuba diving course. Visiting divers are also fast discovering the diverse saltwater and freshwater sites. NZ is at the forefront in establishing marine reserves, where no-take zones have helped depleted marine life recover.

The country comprises two main islands and several offshore island groups. Dive sites span from the subtropical north to the subantarctic south. Warm water washes the Kermadec Islands, where tropical fish swim atop coral in one of the world's largest wholly protected marine reserves. At the other end of the compass

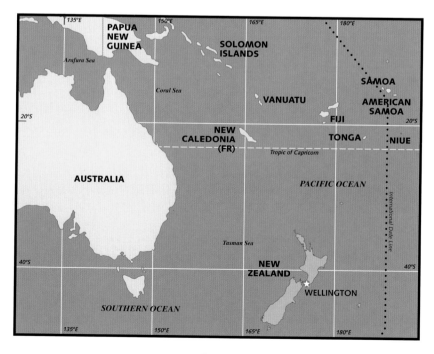

are the Auckland, Campbell and Snares Islands, buffeted by high winds in the chilly Southern Ocean.

Most diving takes place between these two extremes, along the coasts of the North and South Islands, where you'll find massive fish schools, colorful invertebrate life and fascinating shipwrecks. Bathed by the relatively warm East Auckland Current, the islands and headlands of the northeast coast host both subtropical and temperate species. Farther south, kelp forests sway above the seafloor. Along NZ's southwest shores, Fiordland's deep fiords feature a layer of freshwater that cascades from the mountains above and pools atop the saltwater. Tannins in the freshwater tinge the sunlight emerald green and enable such deepwater species as black corals to live close to the surface.

Useful for both residents and visiting divers, this guide presents detailed information on 75 of the best dives in New Zealand, including sites in **Northland**, the **Poor Knights Islands**, the **Hauraki Gulf**, the **Coromandel Peninsula**, the **Bay of Plenty**, the **East Coast**, **Taranaki**, **Wellington**, **Marlborough**, **Canterbury**, **Otago**, **Fiordland** and **Stewart Island (Rakiura)**. Each description includes location, depth range, access and recommended diving expertise. You'll also learn about each site's underwater topography and the marine life you may encounter. Though the book is not meant to be a stand-alone travel guide, the Overview and Practicalities sections offer practical topside information, and the Activities & Attractions chapter suggests ways to spend your idle hours.

Pohutukawa trees bloom in December, brightening much of coastal New Zealand.

Overview

New Zealand is a relatively young country. The first Polynesians arrived about 1,000 years ago, followed centuries later by European explorers, then whalers and sealers, and finally immigrants in search of a better life. Large numbers of Pacific Islanders have moved to NZ in more recent times, and Auckland now boasts the world's greatest concentration of Polynesians. Of NZ's population of about 3.8 million, some 76% are NZ European (Pakeha), 14% are Maori, 5% are Pacific Island Polynesians and 5% are Asian. And yes, there are many more sheep than people— some 48 million, or 12.6 per person.

Geography

New Zealand is 10,400km (6,500 miles) southwest of the U.S., 1,700km (1,050 miles) south of Fiji and 2,250km (1,400 miles) east of Australia, its nearest large neighbor. Stretching 1,600km (1,000 miles) from north to south, the country comprises two large islands, several smaller surrounding islands and a few remote island groups hundreds of kilometers away.

The two major landmasses are the North Island (115,000 sq km/45,000 sq miles) and the South Island (151,000 sq km/59,000 sq miles). Stewart Island (1,700 sq km/ 660 sq miles) lies directly south of the South Island. Most land is undeveloped, as almost 70% of the population live in NZ's five major cities.

Bordered by the Pacific Ocean to the north and east, the Tasman Sea to the west and the Southern Ocean (Antarctic Ocean) to the south, the coast is washed by both warm and cold currents, influencing the weather patterns and supporting diverse marine life.

Geology

The geologic history of both islands is tied to glacial, tectonic and volcanic activity, some of which continues today. About 24 million years ago during the Miocene epoch much of NZ was below sea level, and there was an influx of subtropical plants and marine life, as evidenced by fossilized corals and shells. During the Ice Age some 2 million years ago, water levels dropped 100m (330ft) below today's levels, and NZ was a single island, its southern half largely covered in ice.

Today, the North Island sits along the south edge of a subduction zone, where the oceanic Pacific plate is sliding westward beneath the Indo-Australasian plate. The resulting geologic activity has spawned a number of large volcanoes and thermal zones, as well as vast volcanic depressions, the largest of which is 606 sq km (236 sq mile) Lake Taupo. A rough line of volcanoes, some still active, extends south from the ash-covered slopes of Whakaari (White Island) in the Bay of Plenty. South of Lake Taupo is a trio of volcanically active peaks—Mounts Tongariro, Ngauruhoe and Ruapehu—while far to the west is the volcanic cone of Mount Taranaki (Egmont). Many of the offshore islands are remnants of ancient volcanoes, and Wellington's harbor is a submerged volcanic crater.

On the South Island the geologic process is different. Here the two tectonic plates are smashing into one another, forcing the land upward to form the Southern Alps, which run nearly the length of the South Island. Sprawling east from the foothills to the coast are the Canterbury Plains. Jutting out from the east coast, the Banks Peninsula was formed by ancient volcanic activity and joined to the mainland by alluvial deposits washed down from the Southern Alps.

Geysers dot the geologically active Rotorua region.

History

Maori oral history relates the discovery of the islands in about AD 800 by the navigator Kupe, whose wife, Hine-te-aparangi, named the new land Aotearoa, or "Land of the Long White Cloud." The widely believed story is that Kupe sailed to Aotearoa from Hawaiki (thought to be Ra'iatea in Tahiti), the ancestral homeland of many Polynesians. Tribes tell differing legends, but there were likely a series of migrations in twin-hulled oceangoing canoes. The pristine land and waters

Waka Taua—the Maori War Canoe

Maori war canoes (*waka taua*) are among the most impressive watercraft ever built. Traditionally built from a single kauri or totara tree, the canoes reached more than 25m (80ft) in length and took two years or more to complete. Early European explorers reported seeing fleets of 50 waka traveling together. The sight of such a fleet fully laden with warriors would have been a terrifying sight to an enemy tribe.

Maori boatbuilding skills have seen a revival, with recent canoes reaching 35m (115ft) in length. The hand-carved prow (*tauihu*) and high stern (*taurapa*) showcase the skill of the Maori carvers. Today waka are used for special occasions such as Waitangi Day (February 6) and the Ngaruawahia canoe race in March.

provided these first settlers with abundant food, including ample marine life and birds like the now-extinct flightless moa.

In 1642 Dutch explorer Abel Tasman, who had just circled around Australia from Batavia (modern-day Jakarta, Indonesia), sailed up the west coast of the islands, the first known European visitor. He didn't stay long, though, as his only landing attempt resulted in several of his crew being killed and eaten. He christened the land Niuew Zeeland, after the Netherlands province of Zeeland.

NZ was left alone until British navigator and explorer James Cook arrived aboard the *Endeavour* in 1769, returning in 1773 and 1777. He circumnavigated the islands on the three voyages, mapping as he went, and many places still bear the names he gave them. He made friendly contact with the Maori after he discovered his Tahitian interpreter could communicate with them. Cook claimed the entire land for the British Crown and continued on to Australia.

NZ's first European settlers were temporary—sealers (who nearly wiped out the seal population) and then whalers (who did the same to whales that frequented the coast). Having no immunity to common diseases carried by the Europeans, the Maori population declined dramatically by the 1830s. Firearms trading resulted in the Musket Wars, during which marauding tribes further thinned the Maori numbers.

Around this time European settlers arrived in increasing numbers, some on settlement campaigns organized from Britain. In 1840 the Treaty of Waitangi was drawn up to protect Maori land, fisheries and resources. British sovereignty was proclaimed, and Maori could only sell their land to the Crown.

But the arrival of more settlers led to increased conflict. Known as the Land Wars, or Maori Wars, a series of skirmishes erupted in Northland, Waikato, Taranaki and the East Coast and continued through the late 1800s. Government confiscation of ancestral tribal lands during this period has caused problems ever since. Maori were given the vote in 1867, but continued to lose population and power.

NZ became a self-governing British colony in 1856, a dominion in 1907 and a fully independent country in 1947. Much of the forest covering NZ was cleared for farmland during the colonial period, and farming remains an integral part of the NZ economy, supplying meat, dairy products and wool to Asia, the USA and the UK. Tourism is a growing source of revenue, attracting more than 1.5 million visitors each year.

Visitors can tour several preserved Maori villages.

Diving History

Little recorded history remains of diving around New Zealand prior to 1900. A diver was used in 1863 after the Otago Harbour ferry, *Pride of the Yarra*, sank following a collision. Hard hat divers were also involved in early harbor works and searched for the ship *Elingamite* within days of her sinking in 1902.

One of NZ's first modern-day divers, Leo Ducker began skin diving with homemade equipment in 1946. He explored the Poor Knights Islands in the late '40s using a mask made from a floor polish tin with a plastic faceplate, but no fins. In 1952 he made an oxygen rebreather and dived to 9m (30ft).

A national diving body, the New Zealand Underwater Association, was set up in 1952. Then in 1957, a showing of Jacques Cousteau's movie *The Silent World* inspired many New Zealanders to explore their own underwater world. As the sport grew and diving equipment became more accessible, dive shops sprang up around the country. Formal diver training began in 1963. Most of NZ's early divers focused on freediving and spearfishing.

The *Elingamite* reappeared in the news in 1967, when Kelly Tarlton's photos of the wreck were published worldwide. He and Wade Doak were part of a team of divers that traveled to the Three Kings Islands over the following 14 years to look for remaining treasure. Tarlton would become world-renowned for his treasure-recovery techniques. His final project was the aquarium in Auckland that bears his name. Doak has become one of NZ's foremost marine world experts, with 18 books and two films to his credit.

Today New Zealand boasts the most divers per capita in the world.

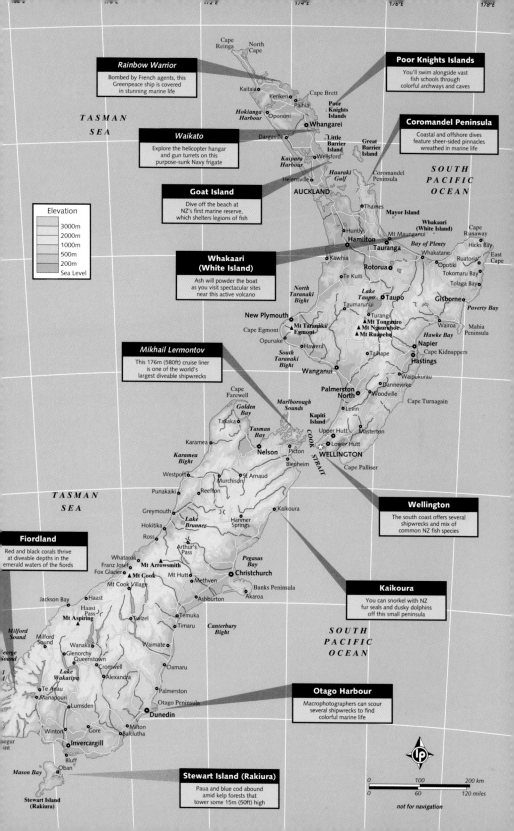

Practicalities

Climate

Lying between 34°S and 47°S, New Zealand is in the Roaring Forties latitude, with prevailing winds from the west year-round. Southerly winds from Antarctica always mean cold weather. As prevailing winds blow from the west, the east coast affords calmer conditions suitable for diving. The country experiences a maritime climate, versus the continental climate typical of large landmasses. This means the weather can change quickly at any time of the year—be ready for sunshine and downpours on the same day.

Summer lasts from December to February and winter from June to August. Conditions are unsettled at the start of summer, with occasional tropical cyclones, which drift south into NZ between December and April. Though they may bring heavy rain and big swells, most cyclones lose their intensity by the time they reach cooler waters. Absent any late-season storms, the weather is generally mildest between February and June, with warm, clear water.

Air temperatures up north range from 15 to 25°C (59 to 77°F) in summer and from 9 to 15°C (48 to 59°F) in winter. In the south temperatures average 10 to 22°C (50 to 72°F) in summer and 2 to 10°C (36 to 50°F) in winter. Parts of the South Island can exceed 30°C (86°F) in summer yet remain below freezing in winter.

Water temperatures vary seasonally from 14 to 23°C (57 to 73°F) in the north and 8 to 18°C (46 to 64°F) in the south. Local water temperatures and visibility are listed in each regional introduction.

El Niño & La Niña

During El Niño years the prevailing westerly winds bring dry conditions to NZ's northeastern coast. The La Niña pattern shifts highs farther south, bringing dry, settled weather to the South Island and Wellington and increased rain and easterly winds to northern NZ.

Language

New Zealand has two official languages: English and Maori. English is the one most widely used, though many places bear Maori names, and use of the language is increasing.

16

Following are some commonly used Maori words you may encounter:

kia ora	greetings/good luck	*moana*	sea or lake
haere mai	welcome	*wai*	water
kina	sea urchin	*kaimoana*	seafood
koura	crayfish	*whanau*	extended family
hiwihiwi	kelpfish	*iwi*	tribe
tamure	snapper	*motu*	island
paketi	spotty	*pa*	fortified village
kai	food	*marae*	meeting house

Getting There

The overwhelming majority of visitors to New Zealand arrive by air. The country's main international airport is in Auckland, though Christchurch and Wellington also handle international flights, and Hamilton, Palmerston North, Queenstown and Dunedin accept direct flights from Australia. Most international carriers or their partners fly to NZ, and there are direct flights from most Pacific destinations.

Entry

To enter NZ you must furnish a passport valid for at least three months beyond your planned date of departure. Australians don't need a visa or permit and can stay indefinitely if they don't have any criminal convictions. British passport holders who can prove permanent UK residency are issued visas on arrival with a visitor permit valid for up to six months. Citizens from most other countries are given a three-month extendable visitor permit upon arrival. If you're unsure, check visa requirements with your local travel agency or the NZ Immigration Service website (www.immigration.govt.nz).

Quarantine & CITES Restrictions

Don't bring any animal or plant species into New Zealand. Enforcement is strict and may include a fine for knowingly breaking the restrictions. Clean any outdoor gear too, as it is also subject to examination.

NZ is a signatory to CITES (Convention on International Trade in Endangered Species; www.cites.org), which restricts trade in threatened species worldwide. Giant clamshells and corals cannot be brought into NZ without a certificate from the Department of Conservation (www.doc.govt.nz). Whalebone, turtle shells, ginseng, caviar and animal skins are all restricted imports and may be confiscated on entry.

Gateway City – Auckland

Auckland is NZ's largest city (population 1.1 million), although Wellington, 485km (300 miles) south, is the capital. Boasting nearly 30% of the country's total population, Auckland is very much the big city of the South Pacific, and its diverse cultures lend it a cosmopolitan air. Most international flights arrive at Auckland International Airport, about 22km (14 miles) south of the city centre. A free shuttle bus runs between the international and domestic terminals. Regular bus service runs between the terminals and downtown Auckland. Door-to-door shuttles and taxis are available outside the terminals.

Nestled between two large harbors—Waitemata to the north and Manukau to the south—Auckland is a great boating venue and is known as the "City of Sails." The city rises from an extinct volcanic field, featuring some 50 volcanic cones, including Mount Eden and One Tree Hill, two of the most scenic overlooks. The most recent volcanic activity, 600 years ago, created Rangitoto, the island just outside Waitemata Harbour.

Take in the city from the Skytower, New Zealand's tallest structure, which includes a 24-hour casino with a revolving restaurant. Visit the New Zealand National Maritime Museum, which overlooks Waitemata Harbour, then take a ferry across to Devonport or a cruise to the islands of the Hauraki Gulf. The fit and daring can take a guided tour to the top of Harbour Bridge. For a glimpse of local culture and history, visit the Auckland Art Gallery and the War Memorial Museum.

A view of downtown Auckland from North Head, on the north shore of Waitemata Harbour.

Getting Around

Domestic flights are available between major cities, with connecting flights to smaller cities and outlying islands. Check luggage weight restrictions when booking your flight.

Regular passenger and vehicle ferries run between Wellington, on the North Island, and Picton, on the South Island. Bus services, including a network of backpacker buses, link most major tourist areas. Limited rail service covers a few main routes. Taxis operate in the cities and some smaller towns.

Car and campervan rentals are popular modes of transportation, especially if you're carrying dive gear. A valid, unrestricted driver's license from your home country is required to rent and drive a car in NZ. Remember, driving is on the left (British style).

Tranz Rail's fast, comfortable trains cover several scenic main routes.

Time

Just west of the international date line, New Zealand is one of the first places in the world to start the new day. The country is two hours ahead of Australian Eastern Standard Time, 12 hours ahead of GMT and 20 hours ahead of U.S. Pacific Standard Time. Ignoring daylight saving time, when it's noon in NZ, it's 10am in Sydney, 9am in Tokyo, midnight in London, 8pm the previous day in New York and 5pm the previous day in San Francisco.

In summer NZ observes daylight saving time. Clocks are set forward by one hour on the first Sunday in October and wound back again on the third Sunday in March.

Money

The local currency is the New Zealand dollar (NZ$). Most banks will exchange major currencies. Major credit cards are accepted by most hotels, shops, rental car agencies and dive centres. Automatic teller machines are widely available.

Almost all goods and services are subject to a 12.5% GST (goods and services tax), usually included in the marked price. Duty-free goods are exempt from GST. Outside of the tourist centres, tipping is neither expected nor encouraged.

Electricity

As in Australia and Europe, electricity throughout New Zealand is on a 230V, 50Hz cycle, with three-pin Australian outlets. You'll need a transformer to use appliances designed for DC supply or different voltages.

Weights & Measures

The metric system is standard in NZ, though the imperial system is still used in some instances. In this book both metric and imperial measurements are given, except for specific references in dive site descriptions, which are given in metric units only. Please refer to the conversion chart provided on the inside back cover.

What to Bring

General

Casual, lightweight clothing is acceptable for most occasions during summer. A wide-brimmed hat, sunscreen and insect repellent will protect you during warmer months. You'll want a warm top for cool evenings and while traveling by boat. A raincoat may also come in handy.

Temperatures drop between April and October, and you'll need extra layers of thermal clothing. Bring a warm hat to wear following a dive. Tramping (or hiking) boots and a rainproof jacket are also useful.

Dive-Related

At the northernmost sites a 5mm wetsuit will suffice during summer, while a 7mm wetsuit or a drysuit is recommended for the rest of the year. In all other areas you'll need a 7mm wetsuit or a drysuit year-round.

Most dive shops rent full gear (except drysuits). You'll need to show your C-card to dive centres and charter operators prior to diving. They may also ask to see your dive logbook. During weekends and public holidays you may need to prebook dive gear and trips.

Underwater Photography

Several dive shops and charter boats rent underwater camera setups. Some dive centres and camera shops also sell a limited range of underwater cameras and equipment.

Most types of film are available in retail photo outlets, although slide film is expensive. Processing labs in many towns offer one-hour print film processing, while E6 processing is available only in the main cities, with delivery service to labs in smaller towns.

Local and visiting divers can contact regional underwater photography clubs in Whangarei, Auckland and Wellington (see Listings, pages 155-156).

Camera setups are available for purchase or rent.

Business Hours

Major shopping centres are open daily from 9am to 5pm, and till 8 or 9pm on either Thursday or Friday. Supermarkets and convenience stores are open daily till 8pm or later. Smaller shopping areas may close at noon on Saturday and remain closed on Sunday. Banks are generally open weekdays from 9am to 4:30pm.

Accommodations

You'll find a variety of accommodations in New Zealand, ranging from campgrounds and cabins to backpacker hostels, farmstays, bed-and-breakfasts, guesthouses, hotels and motels. Book ahead during peak times, which include summer holidays, Christmas and Easter. For more information contact local visitor information centres (see Listings, page 156).

Dining & Food

Main cities offer a range of dining options, from top restaurants that represent almost every ethnic cuisine to brand-name fast-food outlets. Every small town has a fish and chips shop. You'll find fresh seafood in most restaurants, including local fish, green-lipped mussels and red crayfish. Snapper is the most popular fish in the north, while blue cod makes it to more tables in the south. Try local delicacies like whitebait fritters, paua, bluff oysters, smoked fish and mussels.

Traditional Maori food, cooked in an underground oven, or *hangi*, is delicious and usually includes pork, chicken, potato, pumpkin and kumara (sweet potato).

You'll also find plenty of fresh fruit and vegetables in season. NZ has also gained a reputation for quality cheeses and wines, especially white wines. Many vineyards offer tastings and tours.

Shopping

Arts and crafts shops throughout the country offer a wide variety of locally made goods. You'll find beautiful handmade wool clothing, particularly jumpers (sweaters), as well as sheepskin rugs and slippers. Greenstone (jade) and paua (abalone) are made into ornaments and jewelry. Maori artisans carve bone in the shape of dolphins, birds and fishhooks and also carve traditional wooden Maori figures.

You'll find a range of locally made handicrafts in shops throughout New Zealand.

Activities & Attractions

New Zealand offers visitors a variety of land- and water-based activities. The long, winding coastline ensures that no part of the country is more than 130km (80 miles) from the sea. You could spend the morning atop a snowy mountain peak and be lying on a sandy beach that afternoon.

You'll find a host of water-related activities and attractions—from the thrill of a rafting trip down frothy river rapids to the serenity of a coastal sail in the company of bow-riding dolphins. While scuba diving regions may be far apart, there's plenty to do on the journey between. Following are a few attractions to tempt you.

Glass-Bottom Boats

If you want to stay dry and still see marine life, try a trip on a glass-bottom boat. The *Habitat Explorer* (☎ 09-422 6334, www.glassbottomboat.co.nz) operates year-round in the Cape Rodney–Okakari Point Marine Reserve (Goat Island). In summer book a tour out of Whitianga, on the Coromandel Peninsula, or go through the water taxi service at Patterson Inlet on Stewart Island, which also operates glass-bottom boats.

Kayaking

Sea kayak tours offer spectacular scenery and a chance to encounter such marine life as seabirds, seals and sea lions, dolphins and whales. Operators are based in main coastal towns, and tours vary from half- or full-day trips in single or double kayaks to multi-day excursions. Operators provide all equipment—all you need to bring is food and clothing.

Dolphin Swimming

Four dolphin species commonly interact with people. Large grey bottlenose dolphins are found throughout NZ waters. Encountered offshore, smaller grey-and-cream common dolphins often bow ride but are more wary of swimmers. Kaikoura's acrobatic dusky dolphins are very approachable snorkeling companions. At less than 1.4m (5ft) long, Hector's dolphins are the world's smallest marine dolphin. These endangered animals often accompany bodysurfers at Porpoise Bay in the Catlins.

Year-round dolphin swimming trips operate out of the Bay of Islands, Auckland, Whakatane, Kaikoura and Akaroa. Some dive operators also hold dolphin swimming licenses, allowing divers a chance to jump in the water with these playful mammals.

Found in both coastal and offshore waters, bottlenose dolphins often interact with snorkelers.

Whale Watching

You're almost guaranteed to spot whales off Kaikoura. Most often sighted are sperm whales, which feed in deep water close to shore. You'll find them at the surface, catching their breath between dives. When diving, they often lift their great tails clear of the water. Contact **Whale Watch Kaikoura** for more information (☎ 0800-655 121, www.whalewatch.co.nz).

Bryde's (pronounced brood-ess) whales reside along the east coast of northern NZ most of the year. To go in search of them, contact **Dolphin Explorer** (☎ 09-237 1466, www.dolphinexplorer.com), based in Auckland, which offers whale watching and dolphin swimming tours of the Hauraki Gulf.

Orcas, or killer whales (actually the largest dolphin), are frequent visitors, and boaters occasionally spot migratory blue, fin, sei, minke, southern right and humpback whales. NZ's Marine Mammal Regulations prohibit approaching within 50m (165ft) of any whale, and swimming with them is prohibited.

Seal Swimming

Swimming with NZ fur seals off Kaikoura and Nelson can be great fun. Be forewarned, however, that seals are the Jekyll and Hyde of marine mammals. On land they're aggressive and should be given a wide berth. But in the water they'll roll and play with snorkelers and swimmers. Their interest level will mirror your own—ignore them and they'll vanish.

White-Water Rafting

Many of New Zealand's fast-flowing rivers offer the thrill of a raft ride down frothy rapids. Operators provide wetsuits, crash helmets, safety instructions and a skilled guide. Be prepared, as most rivers are snow-fed and often quite chilly— although the adrenaline rush seems to counteract the cold. The most popular stretches of white water are the Shotover, Kawarau and Rangitata Rivers on the South Island and the Wairoa and Kaituna Rivers up north.

Several Rotorua-based rafting companies offer exciting rides down the Kaituna River.

Black-Water Rafting

Black-water rafters traverse underground rivers in rubber inner tubes. Trips vary from a gentle two-hour float beneath masses of star-like glowworms to advanced excursions that involve caving, climbing and rope work. Wetsuits and instruction are provided. If you're unafraid of the dark or enclosed spaces, head to Waitomo Caves on the North Island or Westport and Greymouth on the South Island.

Sailing

NZ is well known for yacht racing, with wins in the America's Cup and Whitbread Round the World Race. But nearly anyone can charter a sailboat. Novices can try organized match races on the Hauraki Gulf with a veteran skipper, while experienced sailors can charter a bareboat and roam the offshore islands in search of their own dive sites. Popular sailing grounds include the Bay of Islands, the Hauraki Gulf and the Marlborough Sounds.

Surfing & Windsurfing

The surf is always up somewhere along the NZ coast. Prevailing westerly winds bring almost constant surf to west coast beaches. When a swell is running on the east coast, the westerlies carve the waves into shapes surfers find irresistible.

Boasting a 2km (1.4 mile) left-hand break, Raglan, in central west NZ, is the country's most famous surfing spot. Surfing conditions are also prime off Gisborne in summer, when Pacific storms stir up big swells and the wind shifts offshore. Other beaches that promise good surf are Ninety Mile Beach in Northland, Muriwai and Piha west of Auckland, Whangamata, Mount Maunganui, Greenmeadows Point in Taranaki, and St. Clair and St. Kilda near Dunedin.

Windsurfers can catch the breezes in Auckland's harbors and the Hauraki Gulf, the Bay of Islands, Oakura near New Plymouth and Wellington. Many beaches provide both surfboard and sailboard rentals.

Swept by prevailing winds, the west coast is where surfers go in search of waves.

Tramping

Many visitors discover NZ's largely unspoiled wilderness along the hundreds of tramping (hiking) tracks that crisscross the country. You'll find the most spectacular scenery on the Great Walks, a series of popular long-distance tramping tracks that take in several national parks. On the North Island are the Tongariro Northern Circuit and Lake Waikaremoana Track, while the South Island boasts the Abel Tasman Coastal, Heaphy, Kepler, Milford and Routeburn Tracks. The Rakiura Track on Stewart Island is the southernmost track. Most tracks are well marked and offer huts for overnight stays.

Several tracks take in Arthur's Pass in Canterbury.

The Department of Conservation maintains the tracks and huts, takes bookings and distributes maps and brochures at local DoC offices. During peak season (January to March) the major tracks can be crowded. If so, have the local DoC office suggest enjoyable alternative tracks. A series of tracks will eventually run the length of NZ from Cape Reinga to Bluff, taking in many of the Great Walks.

For more information pick up a copy of Lonely Planet's *Tramping in New Zealand.*

Kelly Tarlton's Antarctic Encounter & Underwater World

On Tamaki Drive, 6km (4 miles) east of downtown Auckland, this saltwater aquarium is the brainchild and namesake of NZ's best-known diving pioneer and treasure hunter. After strolling through a replica of polar explorer Robert Scott's hut, you'll board a snow cat and cross the ice past a colony of king and gentoo penguins. You'll also tour a series of aquariums showcasing cold-water creatures from the near-freezing Antarctic waters.

Continue via moving walkway through a Plexiglas underwater tunnel amid more than 1,500 of NZ's native marine species. Snappers and kingfish school overhead, as crayfish climb the walls and moray eels lurk in the recesses, baring a fearsome array of teeth. You'll pass through an underwater cave to the next tank, where sharks and stingrays glide effortlessly above you. For more information call ☎ 09-528 0603 or visit the aquarium website at www.kellytarltons.co.nz.

Gentoo and king penguins are a highlight of a visit to Kelly Tarlton's Antarctic Encounter.

Kelly Tarlton

New Zealand's most celebrated diver was Kelvin (Kelly) Tarlton, who excelled at free-diving, underwater photography and spearfishing. He later gave up spearfishing and concentrated on underwater photography, with a focus on natural history and marine archaeology.

Tarlton's photos of the *Elingamite* were published worldwide following discovery of treasure on the wreck in 1967. Tarlton later dived on dozens of NZ shipwrecks, including the *Royal Tar*, *Wairarapa*, *Tararua*, *Tasmania*, *L'Alcmene* and the *General Grant*. He set up a shipwreck museum aboard the bark *Tui*, docked at Paihia in Northland, where bullion from the *Elingamite* and other ship relics are on display.

Tarlton's last project was establishment of the namesake aquarium on the Auckland waterfront. He died on March 17, 1985, the same day he welcomed the 100,000th visitor to the aquarium, seven weeks after opening.

Diving Health & Safety

New Zealand is a relatively safe destination, generally free of unusual endemic diseases or other special health risks. High-quality emergency and medical facilities are readily accessible in most towns.

During summer the NZ sun can be intense. Sunburn is a possibility, even on cloudy days. Use plenty of sunblock, and reapply it frequently, especially after being in the water. Wear a wide-brimmed hat, full-coverage clothing and polarizing sunglasses.

Most health risks associated with diving are easy to prevent or avoid. Keep yourself warm, both in and out of the water. Exercise care on entries and exits, especially at shore sites. Drink lots of water to avoid dehydration.

Diving in a 7mm wetsuit with a heavy weight belt is very different from diving in the tropics. Your buoyancy will change dramatically as the neoprene compresses at depth. Adjust your BC as necessary to avoid rapid descents and ascents.

Dive conservatively. Don't push your depth and bottom time limits. Begin your dive against the current, and finish with a safety stop. Keep track of your position relative to the boat to avoid long surface swims. Don't use up all your air during a dive, especially in kelpy areas—reserve at least 35 bar (500 psi) for the return to the boat. Also bring a dive knife, as old fishing nets and lines crisscross many sites and sometimes entangle divers.

Diving & Altitude

While it's fine to dive soon *after* flying, it's important to remember that your last dive should be completed at least 24 hours *before* a flight to minimize the risk of decompression sickness, caused by residual nitrogen in the blood.

High mountains surround some dive sites in New Zealand, requiring road travel at altitude. If your route takes you above 150m (500ft), consider postponing your return, especially after multiple dives.

Pre-Trip Preparation

Your general state of health, diving skill level and specific equipment needs are the three most important factors that impact any dive trip. If you honestly assess these before you leave, you'll be well on your way to assuring a safe dive trip.

First, if you're not in shape, start exercising. Second, if you haven't dived for a while (six months is too long), and your skills are rusty, do a local dive with an experienced buddy or take a scuba review course. Feeling good physically and diving regularly will make you a safer diver and enhance your enjoyment underwater.

At least a month before your trip, inspect your dive gear. Remember, your regulator should be serviced annually, whether you've used it or not. If you use a dive computer and can replace the battery yourself, change it before the trip or buy a spare one to take along. Otherwise, send the computer to the manufacturer for a battery replacement.

If possible, find out if the dive centre you'll be using rents or services the type of gear you own. If not, you might want to take spare parts or even spare gear. A spare mask is always a good idea.

About a week before taking off, do a final check of your gear, grease o-rings, check batteries and assemble a save-a-dive kit. This kit should at minimum contain spare mask and fin straps, snorkel keeper, mouthpiece, valve cap, zip ties and o-rings. Don't forget to pack a first-aid kit and medications such as decongestants, ear drops, antihistamines and motion sickness tablets.

Signaling Devices

A diver can be extremely difficult to locate in the water, so always dive with a signaling device of some sort, preferably more than one.

One of the best signaling devices and the easiest to carry is a whistle. Even the little ones are extremely effective. Use a zip tie to attach one permanently to your BC. Even better, though more expensive, is a loud air horn that connects to the inflator hose. You simply push a button to let out a blast. It does require air from your tank to function, though.

A great visual device to carry with you is a marker tube, also known as a safety sausage. The best ones are brightly colored and about 3m (10ft) high. These roll up and easily fit into a BC pocket or clip onto a D-ring. They're inflated orally or with a regulator. Some will allow you to insert a dive light into the tube—a nice feature when it's dark.

A dive light itself is particularly versatile. It can be used during the day for looking into rocky crevices and comes in handy for nighttime signaling. Some feature a special strobe option. Consider carrying at least a small light with you at all times—you might go on an unexpected night dive and be glad to have it.

DAN

Divers Alert Network (DAN) is an international membership association of individuals and organizations sharing a common interest in diving and safety. It includes DAN Southeast Asia and Pacific (DAN SEAP), an autonomous nonprofit organization based in Australia. DAN operates a 24-hour diving emergency hotline. DAN SEAP members in New Zealand should call toll-free ☎ 0800-4337 111. DAN America members should call ☎ 919-684-8111 or 919-684-4DAN (-4326). The latter accepts collect calls in a dive emergency.

Though DAN does not directly provide medical care, it does give advice on early treatment, evacuation and hyperbaric treatment of diving-related injuries. Divers should contact DAN for assistance as soon as a diving emergency is suspected.

DAN membership is reasonably priced and includes DAN TravelAssist, a membership benefit that covers medical air evacuation from anywhere in the world for any illness or injury. For a small additional fee, divers can get secondary insurance coverage for decompression illness. For membership details contact DAN SEAP in New Zealand at ☎ 09-445 5036 or DAN at toll-free ☎ 800-446-2671 in the U.S. or ☎ 919-684-2948 elsewhere. DAN can also be reached at www.danseap.org or www.diversalertnetwork.org.

Medical & Recompression Facilities

There are two public hyperbaric chambers in NZ. On the North Island, the Slark Hyperbaric Unit is in the Royal New Zealand Naval Hospital on Calliope Road in Devonport, Auckland. On the South Island, the Christchurch Hyperbaric Unit is in Christchurch Hospital on Riccarton Avenue. In the event of an accident, first call the diving emergency number at toll-free ☎ 0800-4337 111.

For general medical care, refer to a telephone directory in each region. Medical facilities and doctors are listed near the front of the directory.

Medical Contacts

Emergency services
☎ 111

Royal New Zealand Coastguard
toll-free ☎ 0800-262 784
cell phone ☎ *555

Slark Hyperbaric Unit
☎ 09-445 5922

Christchurch Hyperbaric Unit
☎ 03-364 0045

Diving in New Zealand

New Zealand spans a wide variety of habitats, offering dive sites to suit everyone's tastes and abilities. Options range from freshwater lakes, rivers and springs to rocky reefs, towering kelp forests, historic shipwrecks and islands riddled with caves and archways. Adventurous divers can descend in a cage amid sharks off the South Island or delve beneath lake ice in The Remarkables above Queenstown. You can access several sites from shore, while day boats and live-aboards visit dozens of offshore sites.

NZ's waters support healthy corals, though not fringing coral reefs. While you'll spot fewer fish species here than in the tropics, you will find massive schools of fish, especially since the introduction of no-take marine reserves. Rocks, caves, archways and walls are often wreathed with colorful invertebrate life.

The East Auckland Current flows down the North Island's east coast, carrying a variety of subtropical marine species to the offshore islands and coastal headlands. Farther south red, brown and green seaweed dominates, while temperate fish mix with cold-water species, and NZ fur seals are regular diving companions. *Macrocystis* kelp forests flourish from Wellington south, steadily increasing in height to 15m (50ft) off Stewart Island. The cooler waters also support larger paua and common sea urchins. Fiordland's unique waters allow such deepwater species as red and black corals to thrive at diveable depths.

Varying widely between regions, water temperatures and visibility are listed in each of the following chapter introductions. Remember that wind, swell, rainfall and bottom composition all affect visibility, as do plankton blooms in spring and early summer.

Dive Training & Certification

Open Water classes are conducted year-round by dive centres throughout NZ. Courses run about four to five days, including classroom and pool sessions and open-water dives. A medical certificate is required to participate. Divers who have begun a course outside NZ can finish it here through various referral programs. Most dive centres offer resort courses for would-be divers and teach a wide range of advanced certification and specialty courses. Certifying agencies include PADI, NAUI and SSI.

Boat Diving

Most scuba diving in NZ is done by boat, allowing divers access to the rocky reefs that dot the coastline. You'll find boat ramps in most harbors, although some are unusable at low tide. Charter boats visit almost every offshore island. These are usually all-day trips, offering two dives and a surface interval that includes lunch. Some operators emphasize fishing or crayfish hunting, something you should confirm when you book your trip.

Live-aboards travel to some of the more remote areas such as south Stewart Island and Fiordland and offer extended trips to many of the northern island groups. These boats usually accept bookings from groups such as dive clubs or dive shops, though individual divers may be able to book unfilled berths. Make reservations well in advance.

Diving from a kayak is another option. Many coastal dive centres provide self-draining sit-on-top kayaks. Divers wearing full wetsuits will find it easy to paddle, drop a small anchor and dive somewhere relatively unexplored.

A variety of daytrip boats speed divers to offshore sites throughout New Zealand.

Boat Diving Tips

Keep in mind the following precautions when diving from a boat. First, tell someone ashore where you're going and your predicted return time. Commercial operators must always have a boatman on board and display a dive flag while divers are in the water. Don't leave your own boat unattended if you're unfamiliar with the conditions at a dive site. If you do leave your boat or kayak unattended, always ensure the anchor is firmly seated and begin your dive by swimming up-current. Let out at least 50% more anchor line than the depth in which you're anchored.

Shore Diving

Shore diving is often possible along much of NZ's east coast, while prevailing westerly winds often make the west coast undiveable. Beaches are typically a mix of sand and rocks—your best entry point is over sand. While heavy swells may thwart diving at your chosen site, local dive operators can usually direct you to a sheltered site somewhere else along the coast. When diving off the beach, use a float with a blue-and-white dive flag to alert passing boats to your presence.

Freshwater Diving

New Zealand's many lakes, rivers and springs offer diving in crystal clear, though often cold, water. Freshwater diving is a good alternative when heavy swells sweep the coast. You'll need to allow for the lower specific gravity of freshwater and reduce the amount of weight you carry. Diving at altitude will also change your no-decompression dive limits.

Each location presents its own challenges. Many lakebeds are silty and will drastically reduce visibility if disturbed, while spring water is often so clear that it's easy to lose track of your depth. When drift diving a river, divers should be aware of its speed and any submerged obstacles and should arrange for pickup at the exit point. Cave diving is a specialized activity requiring proper equipment and training. Also be aware that remote rainstorms may affect water levels within a cave.

You'll find an entirely different range of species in freshwater, including lake trout, freshwater crayfish (koura), snails, mussels, eels and native fish. Bright green algae coat much of the rocky surfaces, while caves feature dramatic stalactites and stalagmites.

Some of the best lake diving is found at Kai-Iwi, Pupuke, Tarawera and Taupo on the North Island and Te Anau and Wakatipu on the South Island. The most popular diveable springs are Hamurana Springs, north of Rotorua, and Waikoropupu Springs (see sidebar, page 109), near Nelson. Also near Nelson, Riwaka Resurgence is the best-known cave diving site.

Snorkeling

You'll find good snorkeling off most beaches along NZ's rocky coast. The healthiest fish populations are at protected sites such as Goat Island, Tawharanui and Hahei. The reefs surrounding the Poor Knights, Cavalli, Great Barrier, Mercury, Mayor, Aldermen and White Islands also promise good snorkeling, though you'll need a boat to access them. These offshore islands and marine reserves boast huge schools of blue and pink maomao, demoiselles and trevallies.

There are snorkeling trails at Hahei and the Bay of Islands. Snorkelers along Wellington's south coast will spot lots of invertebrate life and juvenile fish amid kelp. You can snorkel with dolphins and fur seals off Kaikoura, Akaroa and Porpoise Bay, while Stewart Island's sandy beaches offer clear water and healthy kelp forests.

Sandy tidal estuaries in the north shelter crabs, mantis shrimp, shellfish, and schooling fish amid nearshore mangroves. The water is usually warmer, calmer and clearer than off the neighboring coast. The best time to snorkel in an estuary is an hour before high tide, when the water is clearest.

New Zealand's Top 10 Snorkeling Sites

Black Rocks (Northland)

Blue Maomao Archway (Poor Knights Islands)

Goat Island (Hauraki Gulf)

Tawharanui Marine Park (Hauraki Gulf)

Kingfish Rock (Coromandel Peninsula)

Orongatea Bay (Bay of Plenty)

Lottin Point (Bay of Plenty)

south coast (Wellington)

Barney's Rock (Canterbury)

Leask Bay (Stewart Island)

Nearshore mangroves offer easy snorkeling and a chance to spot juvenile fish.

Dive Site Icons

The symbols at the beginning of each dive site description provide a quick summary of some of the following characteristics present at each site:

 Good snorkeling or free-diving site.

 Remains or partial remains of a wreck can be seen at this site.

 Sheer wall or drop-off.

 Deep dive. Features of this dive occur in water deeper than 27m (90ft).

 Strong currents may be encountered at this site.

 Strong surge (the horizontal movement of water caused by waves) may be encountered at this site.

 Drift dive. Because of strong currents and/or difficulty in anchoring, a drift dive is recommended at this site.

 Beach/shore dive. This site can be accessed from shore.

 Poor visibility. The site often has visibility of less than 8m (25ft).

 Caves are a prominent feature of this site. Only experienced cave divers should explore inner cave areas.

 Marine preserve. Special regulations apply in this area.

 Decompression dive. This site reaches depths that require single or multiple safety decompression stops.

Pisces Rating System for Dives & Divers

The dive sites in this book are rated according to the following diver skill-level rating system. These are not absolute ratings but apply to divers at a particular time, diving at a particular place. For instance, someone unfamiliar with prevailing conditions might be considered a novice diver at one dive area, but an intermediate diver at another, more familiar location.

Novice: A novice diver should be accompanied by an instructor, divemaster or advanced diver on all dives. A novice diver generally fits the following profile:
◆ basic scuba certification from an internationally recognized certifying agency
◆ dives infrequently (less than one trip a year)
◆ logged fewer than 25 total dives
◆ little or no experience diving in similar waters and conditions
◆ dives no deeper than 18m (60ft)

Intermediate: An intermediate diver generally fits the following profile:
◆ may have participated in some form of continuing diver education
◆ logged between 25 and 100 dives
◆ dives no deeper than 40m (130ft)
◆ has been diving in similar waters and conditions within the last six months

Advanced: An advanced diver generally fits the following profile:
◆ advanced certification
◆ has been diving for more than two years and logged over 100 dives
◆ has been diving in similar waters and conditions within the last six months

Regardless of your skill level, you should be in good physical condition and know your limitations. If you are uncertain of your own level of expertise for a particular site, ask the advice of a local dive instructor. He or she is best qualified to assess your abilities based on the site's prevailing dive conditions. Ultimately, however, you must decide if you are capable of making a particular dive, a decision that should take into account your level of training, recent experience and physical condition, as well as the conditions at the site. Remember that conditions can change at any time, even during a dive.

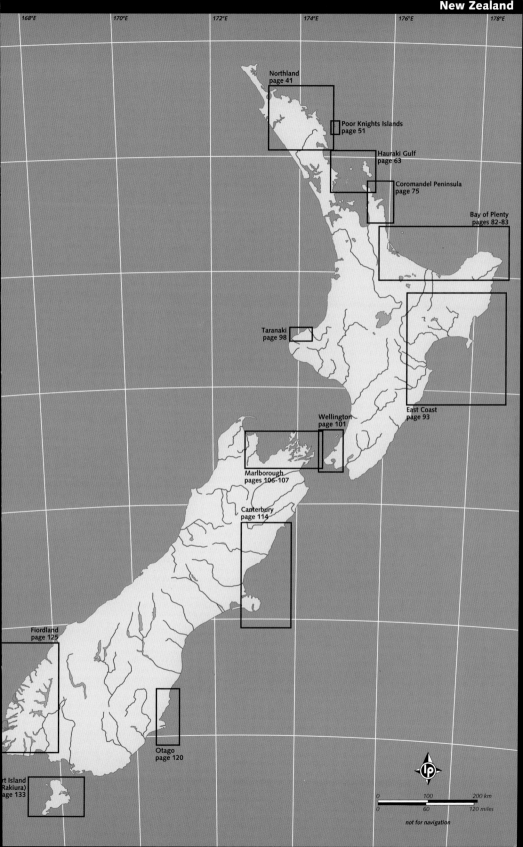

Northland
page 41

Poor Knights Islands
page 51

Hauraki Gulf
page 63

Coromandel Peninsula
page 75

Bay of Plenty
pages 82-83

Taranaki
page 98

East Coast
page 93

Wellington
page 101

Marlborough
pages 106-107

Canterbury
page 114

Fiordland
page 125

Otago
page 120

rt Island
Rakiura)
age 133

168°E 170°E 172°E 174°E 176°E 178°E

0 100 200 km
0 60 120 miles

not for navigation

Northland Dive Sites

Often referred to as the winterless north, Northland is generally warmer than other regions of New Zealand. The Tasman Sea pounds a stretch of sandy beaches along the west coast. Generated by the prevailing wind, big waves limit diving on this coast. But the picturesque east coast features hundreds of beaches, bays, headlands and harbors, with diving and snorkeling along rocky nearshore reefs.

Northland's east coast is dotted with idyllic beaches.

Numerous offshore islands also offer a variety of dive sites, including shipwrecks, pinnacles and deep reefs. Many islands are restricted wildlife sanctuaries—check Department of Conservation regulations before going ashore (www.doc.govt.nz).

A 20-minute drive northeast of Whangarei, Tutukaka is the setting-off point for most charter boat trips to the Poor Knights Islands (see following chapter). The wrecks of the decommis-

Northland Dive Sites	Good Snorkeling	Novice	Intermediate	Advanced
1 Matai Bay Pinnacle	●		●	
2 Taheke Reef				●
3 _Rainbow Warrior_			●	
4 Black Rocks	●	●		
5 Cape Brett	●		●	
6 Danger Rock	●		●	
7 _Tui_			●	
8 _Waikato_			●	

sioned warships HMNZS *Waikato* and HMNZS *Tui* were purpose-sunk as artificial reefs along the Tutukaka coast.

Swirling down from the tropics, the East Auckland Current carries warmer water and tropical species to the Karikari Peninsula, Cape Brett and the offshore islands. Water temperatures reach 23°C (73°F) in summer and drop to 13°C (55°F) in winter. The visibility is usually best between February and June.

Marine mammals are a common sight in these waters. Bryde's whales are year-round residents, as are common and bottlenose dolphins. Orcas, or killer whales, keep a lower profile, slipping into the harbors and estuaries to hunt for rays.

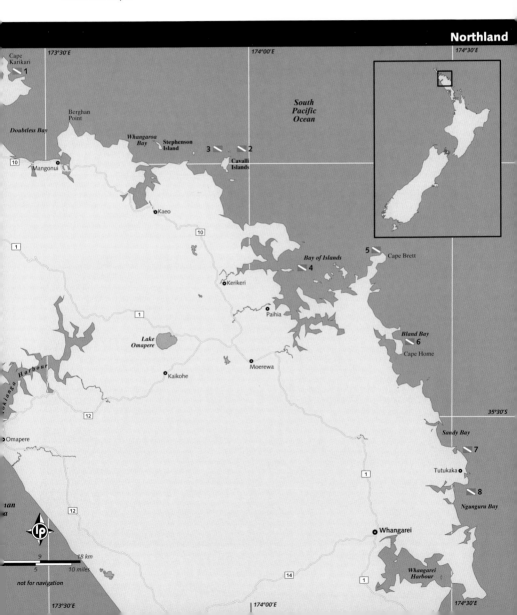

1 Matai Bay Pinnacle

This pinnacle rises above water and is visible from the beach at Matai Bay. It's best dived when the wind is offshore and there's little swell. You'll descend through schools of blue maomao, demoiselles and trevallies. In summer they're joined by predatory kingfish, which hunt amid the schooling fish.

Location: 1km (.6 mile) east of Matai Bay, Karikari Peninsula

Depth Range: Surface-40m+ (130ft+)

Access: Boat

Expertise Rating: Intermediate

Beneath the kelp, jewel and common anemones coat the rocks in a profusion of color. Farther down the wall hydroids and sponges mix with the anemones. Below 15m the fish schools include pink maomao, butterfly perch, mados and a few snappers.

Below the kelp at 25m are a series of sponge-covered canyons, cracks and overhangs. Look closely for apricot nudibranchs, which graze on encrusting sponges and the soft coral known as dead man's fingers. Large crayfish hide deep in the cracks, while strange little Spanish lobsters cling to the undersides of the overhangs. In summer short-tail stingrays spiral around the pinnacle, feeding on Cook's turban shells.

Gorgonian growth is thick below the overhangs. Use your dive light to highlight red *Diadema* sea urchins amid more common black urchins. Deepwater longfin boarfish cruise the walls below 30m, and there's a black coral colony at about 50m near the base.

Sporting distinctive twin spots, a demoiselle darts amid a school of blue maomao.

2 | Taheke Reef

Taheke Reef is best dived at slack tide when there's minimal current. Someone must stay aboard, and all divers should carry a marker tube or similar signaling device. Follow the anchor line to the reeftop, which the waves have swept bare. Schools of trevallies, blue maomao, koheru and the occasional red pigfish surround the reeftop, and packs of hunting kingfish pass through like torpedoes.

Location: 1km (.6 mile) NE of Nukutaunga, Cavalli Islands

Depth Range: 8-40m+ (25-130ft+)

Access: Boat

Expertise Rating: Advanced

Descend the lee side, where you'll find healthy invertebrate life. White hydroids sprout from the walls like bonsai trees. Look for pink *Jason mirabilis* nudibranchs and their matching rosettes of eggs among the hydroid branches. Cracks in the walls are home to very large crayfish and moray eels. Yellow morays are the most common, though you'll also spot mosaic, speckled and grey morays. Watch your buoyancy and depth here, as the walls drop very steeply.

Colorful firebrick sea stars sit amid black sea urchins and the occasional red *Diadema* urchin. You'll find bluefish at around 25m. Look for small schools of golden snappers around the larger cracks and fissures, and check the deeper recesses for rare gropers, including toadstool, spotted black and goldstripe. If you have both wide-angle and macro camera rigs, bring them both. Shark sightings are rare in NZ, but Taheke Reef is a place where bronze whaler, mako and blue sharks or the odd marlin may cruise by.

Lush hydroids and sponges provide both shelter and food.

3 Rainbow Warrior

A mooring buoy marks the resting-place of the *Rainbow Warrior*. Follow the mooring chain down through fish schools until you see the ship's stern from about 8m away. She lies at 25m with a slight list to starboard. Check out the golden snappers near the ship's propeller before heading up to the deck at 15m.

Location: SW of Motutapere, Cavalli Islands

Depth Range: 15-25m (50-82ft)

Access: Boat

Expertise Rating: Intermediate

The encrusted woodwork is covered in kelp atop coarse shell grit, while the rails and hull are coated in colorful common and jewel anemones. Goatfish and leatherjackets fossick for food amid the kelp. Filling the gaps are sponges, bryozoans and hydroids, which conceal tiger and trumpet shells and nudibranchs. Watch where you put your hands, as several well-camouflaged scorpionfish live on the wreck. The dwarf scorpionfish make good macro subjects. Check the dark corners for octopuses and moray eels.

It's easy to become engrossed with the macro life and miss seeing a huge school of kingfish as they swirl silently past you. Inside the hull you'll see thousands of bigeyes, which spill outside the wreck due to overcrowding. Use caution when entering the wreck, as cables hang from the ceilings and silt is easily stirred up.

Schooling fish surround divers on the forward decks, including leatherjackets, snappers, blue maomao, Sandager's wrasses and solitary John dories. The bow pulpit is covered with encrusting life and is the best spot for macro and wide-angle photography.

A patchwork of colorful encrusting life paints the bow pulpit of the *Rainbow Warrior*.

Bombing of the *Rainbow Warrior*

Launched as a research trawler in 1955, the ship was originally based out of Aberdeen, Scotland. She was later bought by the environmental organization Greenpeace and renamed the *Rainbow Warrior*.

In July 1985 the ship was moored in Auckland as activists prepared to protest French nuclear testing at Mururoa Atoll, east of Tahiti in the South Pacific. The French secret service, DGSE, sent agents to stop the *Rainbow Warrior* from sailing. On the night of July 10, two limpet mines exploded against her hull. The first was a warning for those on board to leave; the second sank the ship, drowning Greenpeace photographer Fernando Pereira, who had gone below to collect his camera equipment. Two of the French agents were caught in Auckland, tried and jailed, but the dive team was never brought to justice.

After being refloated, the *Rainbow Warrior* was towed to Matauri Bay, 240km (150 miles) north of Auckland and sunk as an artificial reef in 1987. Now covered in invertebrate life, she has become a haven for schooling fish, attracting divers from around the world. A memorial to the stricken ship (see photo) overlooks the Cavalli Islands at Matauri Bay.

4 Black Rocks

With a maximum depth of 10m, the lagoon at Black Rocks offers good snorkeling and is an easy dive with plenty of fish. When currents pull sediment out of the Bay of Islands, it usually cuts visibility, although in late summer clear blue water washes in. The rocks change to sand at 22m on the seaward side. Schools of small koheru and mackerel attract predators such as kingfish, kahawai and snappers. On the walls amid the sponges and kelp look for red moki and butterfish, while deeper down you'll see butterfly perch and goatfish.

Location: NW side, Bay of Islands

Depth Range: Surface-22m (70ft)

Access: Boat

Expertise Rating: Novice

You'll also find a series of caves, some of which are quite deep. Do not enter them without a guide, as it's easy to get disoriented if the sediment is stirred up. You'll often spot crayfish in the cracks

or at the cave entrances. The walls are covered with anemones, and nudibranchs graze on the encrusting life. Small fish are abundant, filling the swim-throughs and darting around on the rocks and sponges. Look for the larger scaly-headed triplefins, which are bright red when lit by a dive light or strobe.

Nocturnal scaly-headed triplefins keep a low profile by day.

5 Cape Brett

Cape Brett extends some distance out to sea, attracting offshore marine life to its coastline. The best diving is on the north side of the cape, where you descend past kelp forests to sponge-covered boulders. Kingfish and large schools of trevallies, koheru and blue maomao feed at the cape, especially in summer and autumn. This pretty site is well protected from southwesterly winds, though easterly

Location: East end, Bay of Islands

Depth Range: Surface-30m (100ft)

Access: Boat

Expertise Rating: Intermediate

swells can make diving uncomfortable above 15m.

The deep rocky areas shelter fish species rarely seen at other coastal sites, including combfish, crimson cleaners, Sandager's wrasses and sharpnose puffers. Firebrick and yellow Poor Knights sea stars are common, and all five of NZ's moray eel species also dwell here. Shine your dive light beneath the overhangs to spot brilliant red *Diadema* urchins.

Throughout your dive, snappers, pigfish, John dories, leatherjackets, goatfish and demoiselles will swarm around you— look for yellow onespot demoiselles amid schools of twospot demoiselles. Several triplefin species dart over the rocks, making excellent macro subjects. On your return to the surface, check the rock wall closely for a school of blue knifefish that live just beneath the surf.

A diver is no obstacle for shoaling baitfish.

6 Danger Rock

Schools of kahawai, trevallies and blue maomao shoal around the rock as you arrive. You can spend the whole dive on one wall of this massive rock. Every available space is covered in common and jewel anemones. The rock drops steeply to sand and boulders at 25m, then slopes below 30m on the seaward side. Watch for fishing line, and descend below 15m to avoid uncomfortable swells.

Check cracks and fissures along its base for crayfish and yellow and speckled moray eels. You'll find numerous orange, yellow, grey and black encrusting and finger sponges mixed with hydroids and bryozoans. Scorpionfish sit and glare at you from amid the sponges as goatfish fossick in the shell rubble. Look between

Location: Off Bland Bay

Depth Range: Surface-30m (100ft)

Access: Boat

Expertise Rating: Intermediate

the anemones or beneath the black sponges for tiger shells.

Fish schools constantly swirl in to surround you. In summer kingfish add excitement to the dive, as they hunt amid the baitfish schools. While the kingfish are usually small, the baitfish often number in the hundreds. Near the bottom, snappers, butterfly perch and pink maomao mix with individual mados and porae.

7 *Tui*

The wreck of the *Tui* is marked by a series of buoys attached to the bow, mid-section and stern. You can begin your dive at either end and cover the whole 64m ship, which lies on her port side. The superstructure has crumbled away, allowing easy access to the well-lit interior. Just behind the anchor winch at the bow is a large circular hole that leads directly to the decks below. From here you can enter the forepeak or the forward heads and galley. There are more holes on decks one and two, with easy access to the engine room and lower decks. Holes along the starboard hull allow plenty of light into the ship.

More than 50 fish species reside on the wreck, featuring demoiselles, sweeps and blue maomao. A very large school of golden snappers lives inside the ship. If

Location: 4km (2.5 miles) north of Tutukaka lighthouse

Depth Range: 25-32m (80-100ft)

Access: Boat

Expertise Rating: Intermediate

disturbed, these fish make a spectacular display as they stream out through the holes and regroup above the wreck, reentering only when divers have moved off. Wide-angle photographers will find the best vantage point just below the starboard rail near the stern.

Red moki, leatherjackets, porae, John dories and goatfish graze atop the encrusted hull, while inside, bigeyes and slender roughies wait for darkness to feed. Encrusting life includes common and jewel anemones, hydroids, bryozoans, sponges and kelp. Watch your bottom time and ascend one of the mooring lines to your safety stop.

Formerly a hydrographic research vessel for the NZ Navy, the *Tui* was sunk on February 20, 1999.

8 *Waikato*

Buoys mark the *Waikato*'s bow, midsection, helicopter hangar and stern. The purpose-sunk 113m frigate sits upright with a slight list to port. If you descend to the bow section at 28m, you'll find twin 115mm guns and a turret that have broken away from the ship. Snappers sweep over the bow and turret, and the ghostly outline of the bridge towers overhead on the edge of visibility.

A good entry point is the intact aft section, which is wide open with exits along the hull. Only enter the lower decks with a competent local guide or adequate knowledge of the wreck. Alternatively, you can swim along the deck at about 20m to the stern via the helicopter hangar. One propeller is still attached and

Location: 2km (1.2 miles) south of Tutukaka

Depth Range: 8-28m (25-95ft)

Access: Boat

Expertise Rating: Intermediate

shelters a small school of golden snappers. Check holes in the superstructure to find moray eels and crayfish alongside bigeyes and slender roughies.

From the stern ascend to the funnel and the bridge, which is open and easily accessed. Schools of sweeps and blue maomao swim above the ship, while demoiselles and leatherjackets congregate lower down. Kelpfish perch on the crow's nest, and topknot blennies watch your every move. Red rock crabs hide in the niches and cracks on the upper superstructure. Encrusting life covers the wreck, including barnacles, mussels, hydroids, bryozoans, anemones and parchment worms. End your dive at the aft mast, only 8m from the surface and handy to a mooring rope for your safety stop.

The Tutukaka Wrecks

The former New Zealand Navy warships HMNZS *Tui* and HMNZS *Waikato* were sunk as artificial reefs by Tutukaka Coast Promotions.

Launched in 1962 as the USS *Charles H. Davis*, the *Tui* was leased to the NZ Navy in 1970. During 28 years of hydrographic research for the Navy, she was also sent to Tahiti's Mururoa Atoll to monitor protests of nuclear testing conducted by the French government. She was sunk on February 20, 1999.

The HMNZS *Waikato* was one of several Leander-class frigates built for the NZ Navy. She was launched in February 1965 and served until decommissioning in 1998. She was sunk on November 25, 2000.

The following regulations apply to divers on or within 50m (165ft) of the wrecks:

- Divers should be certified in wreck diving
- No anchoring or mooring, except on the vessels' mooring buoys
- One-hour time limit on mooring buoys
- No fishing of any type
- Do not take artifacts or marine life
- Do not damage mooring buoys or chains
- Do not tie up to yellow marker buoys
- Do not litter or discharge sewage
- Follow all other statutory requirements (e.g., 5-knot speed limit, appropriate flagging, etc)

A diver explores the *Waikato*, which reaches within 8m of the surface.

Poor Knights Islands Dive Sites

Twenty-four kilometers (15 miles) off the Tutukaka coast, the islands and rocks of the Poor Knights are the remains of lava domes from ancient volcanoes. Tawhiti Rahi to the north and Aorangi to the south are the two largest islands. South of the main group are the exposed rock faces of The Pinnacles (aka High Peak Rocks) and Sugarloaf Rock.

These uninhabited islands comprise a wildlife sanctuary. Landing on their predator-free shores is prohibited except by permit, usually issued for scientific purposes. The tuatara, an ancient reptile, and the giant weta, likened to a huge grasshopper, are some of the unique species found here.

Declared a marine reserve in 1981, the surrounding waters were granted full protection as a no-take zone in

Diving centres on the spectacular formations.

Poor Knights Islands Dive Sites

	Good Snorkeling	Novice	Intermediate	Advanced
9 Cream Garden				●
10 Northern Archway	●			●
11 Barren Archway	●		●	
12 Middle Archway	●	●		
13 Hope Point	●		●	
14 Landing Bay Pinnacle	●		●	
15 Maroro Bay	●	●		
16 Rikoriko Cave	●	●		
17 Red Baron Caves	●		●	
18 Blue Maomao Archway	●	●		
19 Tie-Dye Archway	●		●	

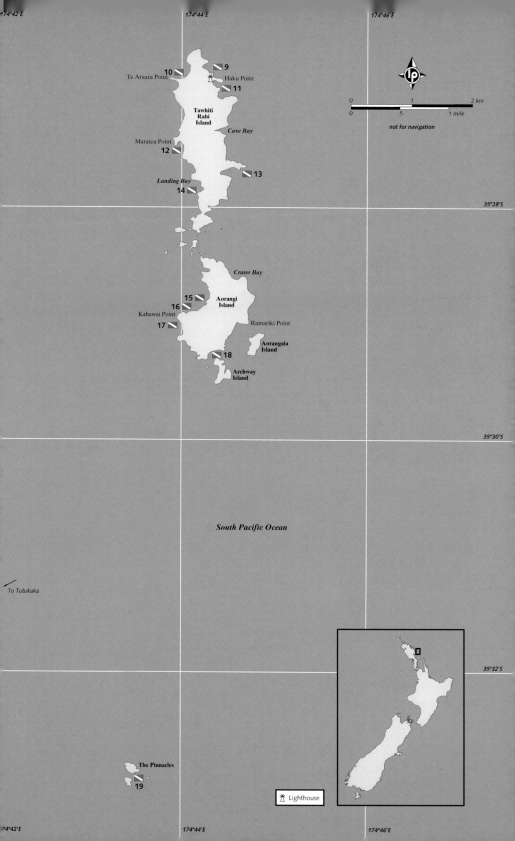

174°42'E   174°44'E   174°46'E

10 Te Araara Point

9

Haku Point

11

**Tawhiti
Rahi
Island**

Cave Bay

Maratea Point

12

13

Landing Bay

14

35°28'S

Crater Bay

15 **Aorangi
Island**

16

Kahawai Point

17 Ramariki Point

**Aorangaia
Island**

18

**Archway
Island**

35°30'S

South Pacific Ocean

To Tutukaka

35°32'S

The Pinnacles

19

Lighthouse

0   1   2 km
0   .5   1 mile

not for navigation

October 1998. Species once subjected to fishing pressures have increased dramatically since creation of the zone, which extends 800m (a half mile) offshore. The East Auckland current sweeps down from the tropïcs, bringing a variety of subtropical marine life. Some species breed and colonize the islands, while others move on at the onset of winter.

The late Jacques Cousteau considered the group one of the top 10 dive sites in the world. Fish-filled caves and archways offer spectacular diving against a backdrop of colorful invertebrate life. The range of depths and dive sites promises something for everyone. Most charter boats leave from Tutukaka, and pickups from Whangarei can be arranged. Boat trips out to the islands average about an hour.

With virtually no runoff from the islands, visibility can reach 50m (165ft) in autumn. Water temperatures range from 23°C (73°F) in late summer to 14°C (57°F) in winter.

East Auckland Current

The warm East Auckland current flows southward along Northland's east coast. Usually encountered out toward the continental shelf, the current moves closer to shore when La Niña weather patterns spawn strong easterly winds. At peak flow the water temperature rises several degrees and visibility reaches 50m (165ft).

During these periods the current brings larval warm-water species to the offshore islands and coastal headlands between Cape Karikari and East Cape. There have been surprising finds of both fish and invertebrates, including lionfish (see photo), surgeonfish, wrasses, cowries, frog shells, *Diadema* urchins and numerous nudibranchs. Regular visitors include turtles, sunfish, manta rays and mahimahi.

9 Cream Garden

You'll descend a vertical wall, passing demoiselle schools atop *Ecklonia* and *Lessonia* kelp forests. Amid the weed below them, scarlet, green, orange and banded wrasses compete with butterfish, black angelfish and marblefish.

Dark overhangs at 20m are the perfect habitat for masses of gorgonians.

Location: NE end of Tawhiti Rahi

Depth Range: 10-30m+ (30-100ft+)

Access: Boat

Expertise Rating: Advanced

Bring a dive light to appreciate the colorful invertebrate life on the wall beside them. At 30m you'll reach a sand platform, beyond which the wall drops below 100m. On the sand are rocks covered in sponges of almost every shape and color, notably finger and golf ball sponges. Motionless lizardfish blend in against the sand, sharpnose puffers hover above the sponges, and colorful mosaic moray eels and a few mottled morays live amid the rocks. Blue mao-mao, porae and demoiselles congregate at cleaning stations run by juvenile Sandager's wrasses, crimson cleaners and elegant combfish. You may also be approached by fearless longfin boarfish, which live below 30m.

Watch your depth on the wall and allow time for a safety stop. If you're shooting macro subjects, save some film for the pairs of banded coral shrimp that wave their feelers from cracks along the wall.

Plunging below 100m, the sheer wall sports clusters of colorful sponges and gorgonians.

10 Northern Archway

Northern Archway is a spectacular dive site. Plan your maximum depth in advance, as the arch bottoms out at 45m. Before descending, swim to the wall and note which way the current (if any) is running. Good buoyancy is essential.

Location: NW end of Tawhiti Rahi

Depth Range: Surface-40m+ (130ft+)

Access: Boat

Expertise Rating: Advanced

Fish that will meet you at the surface include blue maomao, demoiselles and trevallies. Schools of up to 30 large kingfish sometimes cruise through. Below them gather pink maomao, mixed with mados, snappers, porae, red pigfish and leatherjackets. Beneath the pink maomao you'll find colorful splendid perch. Check the dark recesses for golden snappers, toadstool gropers, bigeyes and slender roughies. Near the bottom you may spot yellowbanded perch, spotted black grop-

ers or the rare goldstripe groper. You may also catch a glimpse of timid bluefish up to half a meter long.

The steep walls boast a brilliant array of colorful sponges, hydroids and gorgonians. Mixed in among them are anemones and spiny sea urchins. The sponge life is magnificent, with huge yellow and orange finger sponges beside golf ball, calcareous and encrusting varieties. Search them to find nudibranchs, slipper lobsters, crayfish and morays.

In summer short-tail stingrays fly through the arch, sometimes in squadrons of 50 or more. Bronze whaler sharks are occasional visitors but usually shy away from divers. During your safety stop alongside the wall look for yellow-and-blue Verco's nudibranchs amid the blue bryozoans.

Rays glide through the arch in summer.

11 Barren Archway

"Barren" is somewhat of a misnomer, as the arch supports abundant life. Visit in the morning, when the sun's rays light the interior. A shallow entrance on the north side bottoms out at 12m in a massive chamber. The south entrance is much larger, dropping to boulders that slope from 30m to below the sport-diving limit.

Location: NE side of Tawhiti Rahi

Depth Range: 12-40m+ (40-130ft+)

Access: Boat

Expertise Rating: Intermediate

You can start from either side and swim through the formation, then back via the headland. Only advanced divers should think about diving below the entrance.

Sponge life on the boulders includes yellow and orange golf ball, large black encrusting and yellow finger varieties. Patches of bright yellow zoanthids add to the colorful display. Bring a dive light to appreciate the colors.

Carpet sharks often rest on the boulders in early summer and are safe to approach, as they're not aggressive. Pink and blue maomao, demoiselles and mados congregate overhead. Large scorpionfish perch on the ledges in the main chamber, and halfbanded perch and toadstool gropers hide in the cracks. A face-to-face encounter with any one of the five NZ moray species may boost your adrenaline level.

The east point boasts some of the healthiest *Solanderia* hydroids in the Poor Knights. Inspect them closely to spot grazing *Jason mirabilis* nudibranchs, which lay rosettes of matching pink eggs in the branches.

Sponges include vivid yellow fingers and multicolored golf balls.

12 Middle Archway

From the mooring swim beneath the arch and descend the east span. Prolific fish life includes schooling species and several types of wrasses. Lord Howe Island coral fish cruise in pairs near the bottom, retreating if you approach too close. Several cleaning stations attract demoiselles and blue maomao along with goatfish and porae. Cleaners include juvenile Sandager's wrasses, crimson cleaners, combfish and the odd juvenile trevally.

Location: West side of Tawhiti Rahi

Depth Range: Surface-18m (60ft)

Access: Boat

Expertise Rating: Novice

Both sides of the arch are a mass of color, with various sponges, hydroids, bryozoans, ascidians and some kelp, plus jewel and common anemones. Look amid the blue bryozoans for Verco's and morose nudibranchs. Tiny crested blennies occupy holes in yellow encrusting sponges, darting back just as you press your camera's shutter release.

Delicate gorgonians grow at the base of the boulders alongside large orange sponges. You'll also find yellow and grey morays, sometimes side by side in the same hole.

On the southwest wall is **Bernie's Cave**, its entrance wreathed with gorgonians and its walls coated in colorful sponges. Demoiselles and mados dart about the cave, while porae shelter inside. Check out a small air pocket on the cave ceiling at about 6m. Keep your regulator in place, as the air is likely stale.

A Verco's nudibranch's bright colors warn away predators.

13 Hope Point

Protruding from the east side of Tawhiti Rahi, Hope Point is swept by easterly storms. Its sheer walls host encrusting life and schools of demoiselles, blue and pink maomao and butterfly perch. Large kingfish and porae pass as you descend to the gorgonians and sponge gardens at 30m. Beyond the sand at 37m the wall drops steeply below the sport-diving limit.

After visiting the wall, ascend toward the mooring to find **Air Bubble Cave**, a fine dive site in its own right. To reach the cave from the mooring, swim over the lip of the wall into the recess below. There are three distinct air

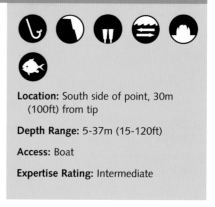

Location: South side of point, 30m (100ft) from tip

Depth Range: 5-37m (15-120ft)

Access: Boat

Expertise Rating: Intermediate

pockets within the cave, each replenished by easterly storms. Ten meters below the surface, the main air pocket can be 60cm high, big enough to accommodate four divers for a quick conversation. Take care when breathing the trapped air, as it may contain high levels of carbon dioxide. Take turns removing your regulators, and if you have any doubts, revert immediately to scuba.

Bring a dive light to find strange little Spanish lobsters that cling to the cave ceiling. On the way in and out check various cracks and fissures for morays eels and toadstool gropers. Solitary corals sprout amid colorful encrusting life beneath the overhangs.

Schooling demoiselles rush to greet a visiting diver in Air Bubble Cave.

14 Landing Bay Pinnacle

Topping out only 5m from the surface, this pinnacle drops steeply to 30m and then gradually to 45m. Big schools of trevallies and blue maomao mixed with demoiselles will surround you at the surface. Farther down you'll find pink maomao, snappers, butterfly perch and tarakihi. Large ocean sunfish visit the bay in summer.

Beneath the kelp down to 25m is an array of colorful encrusting life. Look for blue and yellow nudibranchs on the blue

Location: Middle of Landing Bay, 200m (650ft) from cliffs

Depth Range: 5-30m+ (15-100ft+)

Access: Boat

Expertise Rating: Intermediate

bryozoans. Macrophotographers will appreciate the blue bubble ascidians that cover the walls in spring and summer. In November and December check the slopes for the shell of the paper nautilus, an ancient relative of the octopus.

Look amid black sea urchins to find spectacular firebrick sea stars. *Diadema* urchins shelter beneath the deepest ledges—your dive light will highlight their brilliant red bodies dotted with electric blue spots. Take care when near these urchins, as their spines move rapidly toward any perceived threat and can easily penetrate gloves or wetsuits.

Check the walls for reddish-orange firebrick sea stars.

15 Maroro Bay

This site makes a good second dive, with reefs and sand flats between 5 and 20m. Shallow rocks are covered in sea urchins, sea lettuce and a variety of kelp. Check beneath the rocks for crayfish and Spanish lobsters, which share crawl spaces with bigeyes and moray eels.

Fish life includes butterfly perch, Sandager's wrasses, black angels, snappers, koheru, kingfish and mackerel. Blue maomao, demoiselles, porae, red

Location: West side of Aorangi

Depth Range: 5-30m (15-100ft)

Access: Boat

Expertise Rating: Novice

pigfish and red moki visit the cleaning stations, while John dories hover nearby, waiting to pick off unsuspecting customers.

The rocks are interspersed with sand that gradually slopes to the edge of a steep wall. Sponges grow in plain sight, while hydroids, crinoids and gorgonians thrive beneath the overhangs. Recesses along the base of the wall at 30m shelter red *Diadema* urchins. Rare mollusks such as royal helmet shells and pure white moon shells partially bury themselves in the sand. Remember, this is a marine reserve—take nothing.

In the corner of the bay is **El Torito Cave**, where you can spend

your surface interval snorkeling amid a resident school of blue maomao and demoiselles. Black angelfish nest on rocks just outside the cave, defending their eggs from any intruder.

Black angelfish are rigorous in defense of their egg masses.

16　Rikoriko Cave

This massive cave is large enough for six boats to moor in overnight. If you are on an overnight trip, familiarize yourself with the cave in daylight, then revisit it at night. Novice night divers will appreciate the safe haven in an unfamiliar world. Music from the boat echoes off the walls of this natural amphitheater—you can almost feel it underwater.

Lights from the moored boats attract tiny baitfish and the squid that prey upon them. As you descend the invertebrate-encrusted walls, shine your dive light on tiny solitary corals and colonies of bright yellow zoanthids. They extend their polyps to feed, making this a macrophotographer's paradise.

Yellow, grey and mosaic moray eels venture from their lairs at dusk to hunt.

Location: West side of Aorangi

Depth Range: Surface-25m (80ft)

Access: Boat

Expertise Rating: Novice

Toadstool gropers, bigeyes and slender roughies also feed at night, while pink maomao sleep among the rocks. A school of resident blue maomao moves to and from the cave during the day and forms a protective ball near the back of the cave at night. Red lizardfish perch on the sand near the entrance as sharpnose puffers hover overhead. Look for pairs of banded coral shrimp in the darker corners.

17 Red Baron Caves

Access to the caves is via a series of swim-throughs, and you may exit at any point on the way to the bottom at 25m. When the sun is high overhead, light dances through the many openings like a moving curtain. Wait for calm seas to dive here.

Sponges coat the cave walls in a mix of colors, featuring finger, calcareous, golf ball, cup and encrusting varieties. Hydroids, bryozoans, solitary corals and anemones fill in the gaps. This is nudi-

Location: West side of Aorangi, south of Kahawai Point

Depth Range: Surface-25m (80ft)

Access: Boat

Expertise Rating: Intermediate

branch territory. Verco's and morose nudibranchs graze on the bryozoans, while large predatory green- and yellow-striped nudibranchs hunt for smaller nudibranchs.

You'll find large schools of demoiselles and pink maomao in the caves and along the outer walls. Though porae keep to the boulders, red male pigfish usually venture in for a closer look. Motionless scorpionfish will spread their pectoral fins in a threat display if you encroach on their territory. Photographers should approach slowly for a portrait of their brilliant red patterning.

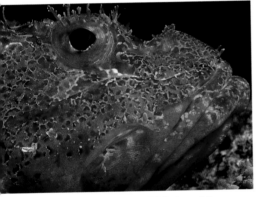

Venomous scorpionfish lie in wait for prey.

18 Blue Maomao Archway

Adjacent moorings in the Labrid Channel, between Archway and Aorangi, mark the east and west entrances to Blue Maomao Arch. You can pass entirely through the arch or exit the way you came. A huge school of resident blue maomao and demoiselles hovers near the larger east entrance. Their numbers fluctuate, but the school is often too dense to see through. Sunlight beams through an opening in the north side, bathing the recesses in sparkling rays. Adding to the magic are yellow and orange encrusting sponges, pink ascidi-

Location: South Harbour, north tip of Archway Island

Depth Range: Surface-15m (50ft)

Access: Boat

Expertise Rating: Novice

ans, golf ball sponges, solitary corals and other colorful invertebrates.

Check the cracks for Spanish lobsters and beneath boulders for big speckled morays. Red pigfish will follow you along the walls, as marblefish cruise amid butterfish, snappers and Sandager's wrasses. Scorpionfish lie camouflaged among the boulders, so watch where you put your hands.

The smaller west entrance is partly blocked by huge boulders. Check your bearings and cross the kelp beds to the channel, where you'll find more mao-mao, koheru, demoiselles and wrasses.

Small kingfish stalk the schools. On the sand near the mooring, red and lilac lizardfish hunt for triplefins, while royal helmet shells occasionally gather to breed.

A large John dory often hovers near the mooring chain and may accompany you to the surface. This overly friendly display isn't all it seems—he's actually using you as cover to ambush swirling baitfish schools.

19 Tie-Dye Archway

Lying exposed to the elements, The Pinnacles cannot be dived in strong winds or if a swell is up. This limited access makes a visit all that more worthwhile, as the area is alive with fish. Descend to the bottom at 25m, where you can best appreciate the immense size of this arch.

Blue maomao and trevallies often wait at the surface. In summer as many as 100 short-tail stingrays cruise the waters around the arch, often gliding in silhouette through light from the east entrances. Photographers' only dilemma will be whether to shoot wide-angle or macro.

The arch was named for the swirls of colorful invertebrate life that paint its walls. Halfbanded perch, triplefins and various shells lie amid the sponges, bryozoans, zoanthids, hydroids, solitary corals and anemones that cover the arch. Various nooks shelter all five species of moray eels, which share space with green and red crayfish.

The black and yellow vertical stripes of Lord Howe Island coral fish will also catch your eye as they move alongside the wall. Golden snappers congregate in

Location: The Pinnacles (High Peak Rocks)

Depth Range: Surface-25m (80ft)

Access: Boat

Expertise Rating: Intermediate

the larger recesses. Usually found below 30m, longfin boarfish often cruise near the edge of the rock platform upon which the arch sits.

A kaleidoscope of colorful marine life graces the walls.

Hauraki Gulf Dive Sites

The 8,000 sq km (3,120 sq mile) Hauraki Gulf contains more than 100 islands and rocks along the approaches to Auckland. Regular ferry service links some of the larger inhabited islands, while many others are restricted wildlife sanctuaries for endangered animals and birds. An exception is Tiritiri Matangi, an open wildlife sanctuary where visitors can wander among endangered bird species. The gulf also hosts resident populations of whales and dolphins.

Underwater the region offers rocky reefs, kelp forests and vast fish schools. Most divers flock to the waters off Goat Island, which have been protected as a no-take zone

Visitors descend on Goat Island Beach in summer.

Hauraki Gulf Dive Sites	Good Snorkeling	Novice	Intermediate	Advanced
20 Sail Rock	●		●	
21 The Canyon	●		●	
22 Simpson Rock	●			●
23 Arid Cove Archway	●		●	
24 Wiltshire	●		●	
25 Ngatamahine Point	●	●		
26 Horn Rock	●			●
27 Goat Island Beach	●	●		
28 Leigh Reef			●	
29 Anchor Bay	●	●		
30 Flat Rock	●		●	

for 25 years. Fish numbers there and at nearby Tawharanui Marine Park are far greater than on the neighboring coastline. In contrast to these beach dives are the offshore sites Sail Rock and the Mokohinau Islands, boasting sheer walls, rich invertebrate life and schools of large pelagic fish. Sites at Little Barrier Island, Horn Rock and Leigh Reef feature undulating terrain, with kelp-covered rocks and boulders that shelter many reef fish species.

Silt runoff clouds much of the coastal gulf, where visibility ranges from 5 to 15m (15 to 50ft), but visibility can reach 30m (100ft) around the offshore islands in late summer. Water temperatures reach 22°C (72°F) in summer, dropping to 13°C (55°F) in winter.

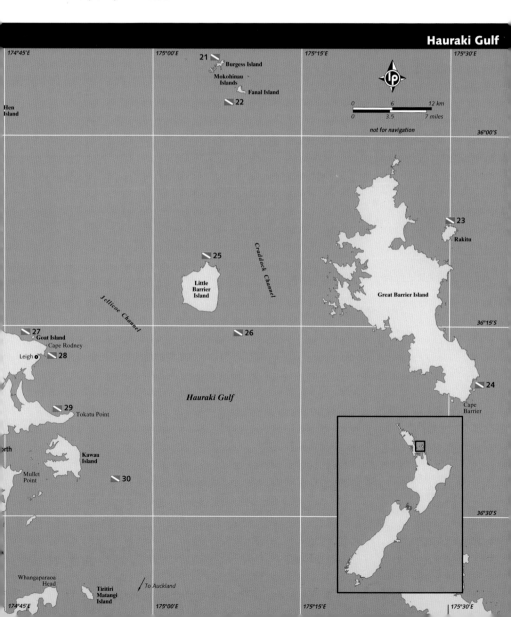

Whales & Dolphins of the Hauraki Gulf

The vast expanse of the Hauraki Gulf is home to large numbers of whales and dolphins. Visitors regularly spot two dolphin species: large grey bottlenose dolphins and smaller grey-and-cream common dolphins. Bottlenose dolphins frequent the shallow coastal waters in pods of 5 to 50 individuals, while common dolphins stay offshore, sometimes in pods of up to 1,000 animals. Both feed on schools of small fish.

The largest and most spectacular member of the dolphin family, the orca, or killer whale, is also a frequent visitor, coming close to shore to feed on stingrays and eagle rays. They form pods of up to 15 animals, often in the shallow upper reaches of Auckland's Waitemata Harbour.

The largest resident mammal is the Bryde's (pronounced brood-ess) whale, also referred to as the tropical whale. Reaching up to 15m (50ft) long, these baleen whales live off the northern NZ coast most of the year.

Other migratory species such as the sei, blue, fin, minke and humpback whales occasionally venture into the gulf. Long-finned pilot whales and small beaked whales known as Gray's or scamperdown whales sometimes strand on sandy beaches along the east coast. The reasons for the strandings remain unclear, though it may have something to do with the whales' social nature and their refusal to abandon a sick or injured companion.

20 Sail Rock

This massive rock towers almost vertically 138m above the surface, plunging underwater to around 40m. The subtidal zone is subject to strong surge. Clear of kelp to nearly 10m, the rock is carpeted in common anemones and sea urchins. Amid them you'll find triplefins, tiger shells, jewel anemones and small scorpionfish, all of which make good macrophotography subjects.

Schools of trevallies, sweeps and blue maomao cruise near the surface along with mackerel, koheru and kingfish. As you descend, swarms of demoiselles sur-

Location: SW of Hen Island

Depth Range: Surface-40m (130ft)

Access: Boat

Expertise Rating: Intermediate

round you and schools of silver drummers swirl in to feed on the kelp. Large cracks and fissures and scattered boulders shelter several species of trumpet shells and both red and packhorse crayfish. Also look for resident red moki and yellow moray eels. Snappers, tarakihi, leatherjackets, porae and John dories graze the slopes below 20m amid a variety of sponges.

The blue water and large fish schools make this a magical dive. Bring a dive knife, as you may encounter tangled fishing line amid the kelp.

21 The Canyon

A spectacular dive, The Canyon is what remains of a sea cave with a collapsed ceiling. From the mouth of the canyon, drop to the bottom at 30m and work your way in beside the wall. Expect to be buzzed by schooling fish. Kingfish, trevallies and blue maomao congregate at the mouth, while below them pink maomao schools mix with butterfly perch and the occasional brilliantly colored splendid perch. Farther in, snappers, pigfish, Sandager's wrasses, silver drummers and masses of demoiselles blend with the maomao schools.

Location: NW side of Burgess Island, Mokohinau Islands

Depth Range: Surface-30m (100ft)

Access: Boat

Expertise Rating: Intermediate

Bring a dive light to search the small caves and cracks for yellow morays and small crayfish. Wreathing the cave entrances are colorful feather stars and crinoids in yellow, brown and sometimes red. Look amid the boulders on the bottom for well-camouflaged scorpionfish and lizardfish.

Macrophotographers will find plenty of subjects. The canyon walls are covered with such colorful invertebrates as sponges, hydroids, bryozoans and jewel anemones. Several striking nudibranch species nibble on the invertebrates. Marine life thrives in the shallows, giving you plenty to check out during your safety stop.

Jason mirabilis nudibranchs are voracious carnivores.

22 Simpson Rock

Simpson Rock was once a military target, and there are unexploded shells on the seafloor. Do not handle or attempt to bring any to the surface. Although the rock is small, the terrain varies from east to west. Enter on the east side, where you'll encounter snappers, trevallies, butterfly perch and demoiselles. A crack near the centre of the rock becomes a cave at 20m. Near the cave entrance at 25m is a level platform that gradually drops below the sport-diving limit.

Location: Southernmost rock of the Mokohinau Islands

Depth Range: Surface-30m (100ft)

Access: Boat

Expertise Rating: Advanced

You'll find scorpionfish and large red moki amid the sponge-covered boulders. Bigeyes and slender roughies congre-

A scorpionfish blends in well atop the boulders.

gate beside boulders that conceal yellow moray eels. This is another good macro dive, with plenty of nudibranchs, ascidians and anemones.

The current is stronger and the visibility reduced on the west side. Masses of fish feed in the current, notably blue and pink maomao and trevallies. You may spot blue moki amid the schooling fish. Larger predators, such as kingfish and the occasional bronze whaler shark, prey on schools of baitfish. Keep close to the rock and out of the current, as choppy surface conditions make spotting a diver in open water difficult. The safest ascent is on the east side.

23 Arid Cove Archway

Part of a proposed marine reserve on the northwest side of Arid Cove, this site offers something for everyone. Start by swimming down the sheer wall outside the arch to the sponge gardens. Fish life is prolific, and the demoiselle schools will quickly surround you. Large yellow and grey finger sponges grow amid smaller sponges. Yellow moray eels often drape themselves over black sponges among the boulders.

Location: West side of Rakitu, NE of Great Barrier Island

Depth Range: 3-30m (10-100ft)

Access: Boat

Expertise Rating: Intermediate

On your way up you may pass kingfish as they stalk the baitfish, especially in summer and autumn. Continue up and over the kelp forest into the archway. John dories hunt small fish near the kelp forest, as red pigfish move in close to inspect divers. Large blue moki often hover in the gap, surrounded by sweeps, demoiselles, blue maomao, butterfly perch, koheru and jack mackerel. Little

halfbanded perch rest on ledges within the arch.

Sponges, solitary corals, bryozoans, hydroids and anemones coat the walls of the arch, and schooling fish are silhouetted against a shimmering curtain of sunlight. Photographers will be happy with both wide-angle and macro setups.

24 | *Wiltshire*

This 150m steamship sank during a storm after hitting rocks near Rosalie Bay in May 1922. The ship broke in two, her stern section coming to rest alongside the bow. Although portholes and other fixtures are long gone and the wreck has broken up, it's still a good dive. Visibility is best in late summer and autumn. Dive here when the wind is out of the northwest and there's no easterly swell.

Start your dive deep amid the broken midsection and work toward the shallows. Chunks of the hull, superstructure

Location: Rosalie Bay, 5km (3 miles) NE of Cape Barrier, Great Barrier Island

Depth Range: 3-30m (10-100ft)

Access: Boat

Expertise Rating: Intermediate

and machinery lie scattered across the reef. Swarming over the deeper sections are snappers, tarakihi, leatherjackets and

Divers will find scarlet wrasses and dozens of other species on the *Wiltshire*.

blue maomao. Kingfish stalk big schools of baitfish.

Look beneath the wreckage to find crayfish, yellow morays and conger eels.

Colorful tiger and trumpet shells nestle among the sponges and anemones, while octopuses discard empty shells in a neat half-circle around their lairs.

25 Ngatamahine Point

A permit is required to land on Little Barrier Island, which serves as a sanctuary for some of New Zealand's endangered wildlife. Underwater a series of pinnacles drops steeply to 25m, the channels between them sheltering large schools of fish and a range of grey and orange finger sponges. You'll swim among butterfly perch, pink maomao, small snappers, trevallies, blue maomao and sweeps.

Large numbers of red moki share space with crayfish and the occasional Spanish lobster in the nooks between boulders. Rarer painted moki usually swim singly or in pairs above the kelp. In summer months you may spot a dozen or more longtail stingrays and eagle rays resting on sand amid the kelp.

Location: NE point, Little Barrier Island

Depth Range: 10-25m (35-80ft)

Access: Boat

Expertise Rating: Novice

Macrophotographers are at home here. Amid the anemones on the vertical walls are trumpet and tiger shells, arguably the most attractive NZ gastropods. Also keep an eye out for large resident yellow moray eels. Octopuses hide in the cracks, while broad squid hunt atop the kelp. Look for bunches of fingerlike white egg masses left by the mating squid.

26 Horn Rock

Begin your dive by descending the anchor rope at slack water. The rock breaks the surface, and the sandy floor ranges from 15 to 25m between the walls of the rocky reef. On calm days fish school at the surface, and you'll descend through blue maomao, sweeps, demoiselles, trevallies, kahawai and kingfish. Toward the bottom you'll find butterfly perch and silver drummers.

Luxuriant kelp growth covers most of the rocky areas. In late summer the kelp conceals large numbers of often bright red goatfish. John dories linger near the kelp, where red moki also fossick for food.

Location: SE of Little Barrier Island

Depth Range: 10-25m (30-90ft)

Access: Boat

Expertise Rating: Advanced

Check cracks between rocks to spot crayfish feelers. *Jason mirabilis* nudibranchs graze amid jewel anemones and white bonsai-like hydroids that line the walls.

Large eagle rays and short- and longtail stingrays often settle on the sand—

the largest more than 4m from nose to tip of tail. If a ray feels threatened, it will lift its tail and wings. Once you back off, it will typically settle back down.

If the current picks up during your dive, remember to swim into it, or you may end up a long way from your dive boat. To be safe, bring a marker tube.

Bottom-dwelling goatfish seek shelter amid the kelp holdfasts at Horn Rock.

27 Goat Island Beach

Established in 1975, the Cape Rodney–Okakari Point Marine Reserve, better known as Goat Island, was NZ's first marine reserve. Unload your dive gear in the five-minute zone close to the beach before heading to the main car park. During summer it's best to arrive early, as the beach can get crowded. Enter from the sand and swim toward Shag Rock, about 200m from shore. The best time to dive is at high tide, when fish move in closer to the beach.

As you enter the water, blue maomao, snappers and parore surround you. Early risers will be accompanied by literally

Location: 3km (1.9 miles) NW of Leigh, NE of Warkworth

Depth Range: Surface-15m (50ft)

Access: Boat or shore

Expertise Rating: Novice

hundreds of fish. Don't feed them, as the fish become unnaturally aggressive. Eagle rays often pass close to the beach, though they move to deeper water when crowds are largest.

Large schools of silver drummers and big snappers descend on Shag Rock at high tide. Look amid the kelp to find butterfish, blue cod, banded wrasses, red moki and, of course, kelpfish. Check darker corners for large crayfish. Schools of two-spot demoiselles and several yellow moray eels stick to the north end of the island. As the seafloor slopes to 15m, the kelp mixes with encrusting and finger sponges.

In summer giant boarfish, normally found at depths below 15m, feed atop the sandy patches near Shag Rock. Pipers hover near the surface, while broad squid shuttle over the kelp. The benefits of no-take marine reserves are evident, as fish and crayfish are thriving.

Just offshore from Goat Island Beach, Shag Rock is home to large schools of silvery snappers.

28 Leigh Reef

Although heavily fished, Leigh Reef still boasts plenty of fish and invertebrate life. About 500m east of The Outpost (Panetiki) at the entrance to Leigh Harbour, the reef covers more than a square kilometer and is often visited by a fleet of dive boats. It's best dived at slack water, as there's usually a current. A knowledgeable captain is a must.

Location: 1km (.6 mile) east of Leigh Harbour

Depth Range: 12-25m (40-80ft)

Access: Boat

Expertise Rating: Intermediate

Descend via the anchor rope to the reef between 15 and 20m, well below any surface surge. You'll pass schools of mackerel, sweeps and blue maomao near the surface and butterfly perch and demoiselles farther down. Mados, red moki and goatfish stick close to the reef, while giant boarfish skirt the sand at the edge of the reef.

Bring a dive light, as the site is riddled with caves and swim-throughs. Never lose sight of the cave entrances and be careful not to disturb silt, which will cloud visibility. Schools of bigeyes move aside as you enter the caves. Crayfish, yellow morays and large conger eels live toward the back of some caves.

The outer walls are covered in encrusting sponges, jewel and common anemones, dead man's fingers and hydroids. Large black and purple sponges fill the gaps between the orange and grey finger sponges, and you may find the occasional sand or spiny sea star. Peer around the kelp holdfasts to find goatfish. Schools of kingfish, some more than a meter long, make close passes in summer.

Drift Diving Tips

Drift diving is an excellent way to use a current to cover a large area with minimal effort. Plan your dive carefully, checking tide charts, the direction of the current and any hazards that may be encountered on the dive. A signaling device is a must—each diver should carry a whistle or signal marker, preferably both. Choose a dive operator with good local knowledge to keep track of you from the surface.

You should be an experienced diver, able to descend without a line and equalize your ears quickly. Underwater, you must maintain buddy contact and be able to do a safety stop without a reference line while maintaining neutral buoyancy.

Sea stars typically boast anywhere from five to more than a dozen arms.

29 Anchor Bay

If you're carrying gear, the entry point is a long walk from the car park. You may prefer to visit by boat, though rocky reefs along the beach offer good snorkeling. Diving conditions are best in a southwest or southerly wind.

Location: Tawharanui Marine Park

Depth Range: Surface-15m (50ft)

Access: Boat or shore

Expertise Rating: Novice

From the beach head east toward a rock platform known as Flat Rock. From here the sandy bottom slopes gently and blends with the reef. Below 10m sponges sprout amid the kelp. You'll find leatherjackets, spotties, snappers, red moki, John dories, banded wrasses and goatfish. Large crayfish abound under the rocks and ledges, benefiting from the no-take zone established in 1980. They share their lairs with large red moki and the occasional yellow moray eel. Look for a crescent of discarded shells amid the rocks and you may find an octopus in residence.

In summer blue maomao and sweeps form large schools, accompanied by jack mackerel and kahawai. Snappers are still wary, but their numbers are increasing. The steeply sloping reefs to the east boast more sponge growth. Eagle rays and short- and longtail stingrays rest on the sand between reefs.

With eyesight rivaling our own, an octopus posts watch over its stack of discarded shells.

30 Flat Rock

Flat Rock is easy to find, as it's marked with two prominent navigation lights. Currents carry silt from the inner gulf, often reducing visibility. Dive here at slack water, either at the top or bottom of the tide. When a northeast swell is running, descend on the lee side of the rock. Ensure that your boatman is aware of your dive profile and ready to pick you up should you drift off the site. The reef is heavily fished, so bring a sharp knife to cut through fishing line.

Descend via the anchor rope through schools of sweeps, blue maomao and trevallies to the sandy bottom between rocky reefs. Large skittish snappers feed in the sand gullies, while John dories move right in to hunt small fish that school around you.

Location: East of Kawau Island

Depth Range: Surface-15m (50ft)

Access: Boat

Expertise Rating: Intermediate

Various nooks house large red and occasionally green crayfish. Beneath the thick kelp beds are myriad common and jewel anemones, triplefins, encrusting sponges and hydroids. Look between the reefs for beautiful dahlia anemones and sand stars and on the nearby rocks for giant seven-armed sea stars. Stingrays and eagle rays are common, especially in summer, when you may also spot large kingfish and kahawai.

Calling to mind a peacock's tail, a bold "eye" stares out from the flanks of a John dory.

Coromandel Peninsula Dive Sites

Stretching 100km (60 miles) south to north, the Coromandel Peninsula divides the Hauraki Gulf from the Bay of Plenty. The best dive sites are off the east coast of the peninsula amid scattered islands, the remnants of ancient volcanoes.

Marine life is protected within Cathedral Cove.

The region's invertebrate life and kelp-covered boulder banks are similar to those found in the Poor Knights Islands, though you should expect fewer fish. Best accessed from Whitianga, the Mercury Islands boast large reefs. Farther south, off Tairua, are the Aldermen Islands, which offer steep-walled pinnacles.

There are also spectacular nearshore dive sites around the headlands, inshore reefs and pinnacles. The best of these is the Te Whanganui-A-Hei Marine Reserve, more commonly known as Hahei or Cathedral Cove. Fish life thrives in the protection of the marine reserve. The diving is spectacular near the reserve boundary, and a snorkeling trail at the north end covers most of the coastal habitats.

Reduced by heavy rains and runoff, visibility on the coast tops out at 20m (65ft), while visibility around the islands sometimes exceeds 30m (100ft). Water temperatures reach 21°C (70°F) in summer and drop to 12°C (54°F) in winter.

Coromandel Peninsula Dive Sites	Good Snorkeling	Novice	Intermediate	Advanced
31 Never Fail Reef	●		●	
32 Kingfish Rock	●	●		
33 South Sunk Rock	●		●	
34 The Gardens	●	●		
35 McGregor's Pinnacle	●			●
36 Rat Rock	●		●	

74

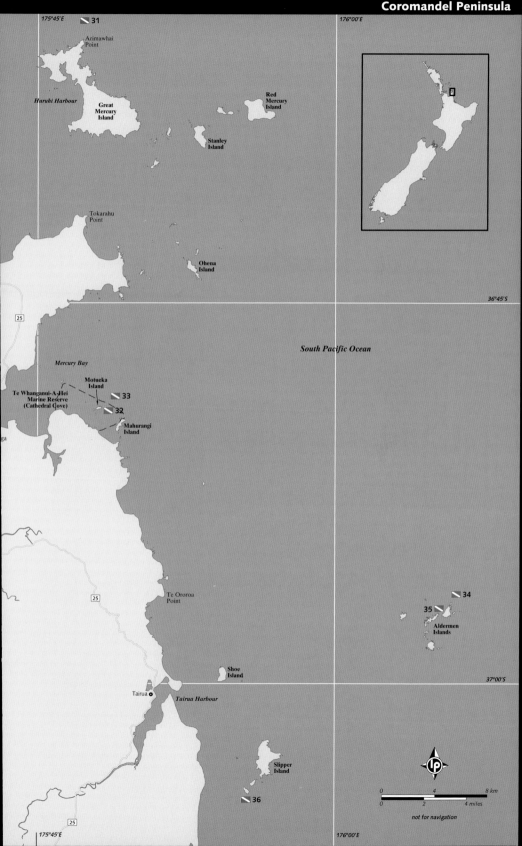

175°45'E

31

Arimawhai
Point

Huruhi Harbour

Great
Mercury
Island

Red
Mercury
Island

Stanley
Island

176°00'E

Tokarahu
Point

Ohena
Island

36°45'S

25

South Pacific Ocean

Mercury Bay

Motueka
Island

Te Whanganui-A-Hei
Marine Reserve
(Cathedral Cove)

33

32

Mahurangi
Island

ga

25

Te Ororoa
Point

34

35

Aldermen
Islands

Shoe
Island

37°00'S

Tairua

Tairua Harbour

Slipper
Island

25

36

0   4   8 km

0   2   4 miles

not for navigation

175°45'E

176°00'E

Hot Water Beach

After a dive at Hahei, head south to Hot Water Beach and dig your own natural hot tub (two hours before or after low tide). The hot water comes from a deep underground spring that passes near a volcanic vent, heating the water. If you get too hot, take a cool dip in the ocean. Be careful if there's heavy surf, though, as several people have drowned.

LAURENCE BELCHER

31   Never Fail Reef

As at most of the Mercury Islands, this site is best dived when the wind is from the southwest. The rock wall drops quickly, so watch your depth and the currents here. Kelp covers the rock down to 20m, where you'll be below the surge zone. You'll find scarlet and banded wrasses, butterfish, John dories, sweeps, demoiselles and red moki. The kelp holdfasts and surrounding terrain are a macrophotographer's dream, supporting hydroids, compound ascidians, solitary corals, sponges and nudibranchs.

Location: 1km (.6 mile) off north tip, Great Mercury Island

Depth Range: Surface-33m (110ft)

Access: Boat

Expertise Rating: Intermediate

Yellow moray eels and big crayfish fill the crevices, including the rarer green, or packhorse, crayfish. Fish schools abound, featuring trevallies, kahawai and baitfish. In summer big kingfish round the baitfish into balls and smash through them, picking off the stragglers. Sponges abound below the kelp. Butterfly perch, demoiselles, snappers, tarakihi and porae feed beneath schools of pink maomao.

Spend your safety stop along the wall in the kelp zone. Resident species include several types of nudibranchs. Tiger shells are also common, and the chocolate-and-white shell of the NZ trumpet glows from deep within the reef nooks. The orange animal itself makes a great photo subject when extended to feed on sea stars.

Save some film to capture colorful invertebrate life in the kelp zone at Never Fail Reef.

32 Kingfish Rock

Kingfish Rock is an underwater pinnacle within Te Whanganui-A-Hei (Cathedral Cove) Marine Reserve. Visible from the surface, the peak is covered with common anemones interspersed with jewel anemones and kelp. As you descend the wall, schools of sweeps, blue maomao, demoiselles and mackerel give way to red moki, leatherjackets, spotties, butterfish and scarlet and banded wrasses.

Off the east side is a smaller pinnacle at 15m, the 5m gap between them fringed with hydroids that extend from both walls. Below 12m black and bright

Location: 1.5km (.9 mile) off Hahei Beach, between Motueka & Mahurangi

Depth Range: 5-23m (15-75ft)

Access: Boat

Expertise Rating: Novice

yellow encrusting sponges cover the rocks. Amid them you'll find grey finger and purple cup sponges. The glowing white polyps of orange soft corals, or dead man's fingers, are mixed with bryozoans and ascidians.

Large snappers, John dories, scarlet wrasses and blue cod shadow divers at the base of the pinnacle. Big schools of jack mackerel swirl down from the surface, often followed by the kingfish that prey on them.

Short-tail stingrays flock here for Cook's turban shells, their favorite food. Check reef nooks for crayfish, which are bigger and more plentiful since the creation of the no-take reserve. Red cod and redbanded perch share space with the crayfish, and triplefins are posted at the openings. Leatherjackets offer a diversion during your safety stop as they feed on encrusting life. Be wary of strong surge atop the rock.

Kingfish Rock is capped with common and jewel anemones.

33 South Sunk Rock

South Sunk Rock sits just outside the Te Whanganui-A-Hei (Cathedral Cove) Marine Reserve. It covers a large area of rocky terrain between 10 and 15m, with several high spots that just break the surface. The walls drop to boulders at 20m, below the surge zone, then slope to 30m onto sand.

Location: North of Mahurangi Island

Depth Range: Surface-30m (100ft)

Access: Boat

Expertise Rating: Intermediate

Surrounded by white anemones, large green-lipped mussels fill the reeftop. Remember, it's illegal to take mussels on scuba. Swim down to an undulating seascape through blue maomao, sweeps, demoiselles, snappers and tarakihi. Deep canyons are lined with sponges, hydroids and ascidians. Kelp growth is also healthy, providing a haven for smaller fish.

You'll see lots of brown-patterned marblefish, which are very approachable. Watch as they grab a mouthful of weed, let the surge tear it away, then settle down to swallow it. You'll also find scarlet, orange and banded wrasses, spotties, redbanded perch, black angelfish, leatherjackets, red moki, scorpionfish and short-tail stingrays. In summer and fall packs of hungry kingfish flash through tight balls of baitfish.

Yellow moray eels are common, peering from their lairs with gaping mouths.

The largest ones grow to 1.5m. Check for crayfish and the odd Spanish lobster in the deeper crevices. Macrophotographers will find plenty of other subjects.

Check reef crevices to find yellow moray eels.

34 The Gardens

The Gardens makes a great second dive following a visit to the deeper reefs. From the boat you'll drop into a kelp forest capped with schooling demoiselles and blue maomao. The kelp sways back and forth in the surge. The bottom is a mass of boulders, some very large. Check beneath these for crayfish, which share space with very large red moki. Don't

Location: West side of George Island, Aldermen Islands

Depth Range: Surface-20m (65ft)

Access: Boat

Expertise Rating: Novice

be surprised if you also spot one or more yellow moray eels.

Resplendent red goatfish root along the bottom for food with accompanying spotties, which dart in to steal food the goatfish uncover. You'll also find lots of colorful sponges, ascidians and hydroids. Lovely dahlia anemones extend their tentacles atop the sand between rocks. This large species ranges in color from patterned red to brownish-orange. Covering the rocks are their cousins, jewel and common anemones, between which flit small triplefins.

Fishing pressures keep the few snappers here fairly small. Beware of the occasional fishing line and hooks entangled in the kelp.

As you drift over The Gardens, look for the beautiful "blooms" of dahlia anemones.

35 McGregor's Pinnacle

One of several sites near George Island, this dive is typical of the pinnacles at the Aldermen Islands. Its sheer walls are laden with sponges and hydroids, with sparse kelp higher up in the surge zone. You'll descend through huge schools of kingfish and trevallies, pink maomao and butterfly perch. Note the direction of the current and stay close to the pinnacle.

Location: 1km (.6 mile) NE of George Island, Aldermen Islands

Depth Range: 8-30m (25-100ft)

Access: Boat

Expertise Rating: Advanced

Shocks of long yellow finger sponges sprout from the pinnacle's sheer walls.

On a clear day in late summer, this dive is among the best in NZ, with common sightings of sharks and marlin. Schooling fish fill the water from the surface to the rocky reef floor. Red moki, pigfish, leatherjackets and butterfly perch move above the yellow and grey finger sponges, golf ball sponges, hydroids and ascidians. Demoiselles surround you in number at any depth, and beneath the pink maomao you may spot a brightly colored splendid perch.

Spend your safety stop atop the pinnacle, saving film for shots of nudibranchs and triplefins. Both packhorse and large red crayfish fill the crevices.

36 | Rat Rock

Rat Rock offers little shelter and is only diveable absent any wind or swell. If the boat is anchored close to the rock, follow the line down to 20m and work your way around to the shallows, swimming into the current. Kelp-covered rocks sit amid sand patches along the bottom. Resident fish include butterfly perch, tarakihi, spotties, banded and scarlet wrasses, leatherjackets and the occasional John dory.

The rocks boast healthy sponge growth, and you'll find many live shells and nudibranchs. Look for several large tiger shells attached to the prevalent grey finger sponges. Crayfish and yellow moray eels fill the crevices.

Location: South end of Slipper Island

Depth Range: Surface-20m (65ft)

Access: Boat

Expertise Rating: Intermediate

Common and jewel anemones cover the walls around 12m. Check the cracks for large red moki and small caves for more crayfish. Kingfish often visit in summer to hunt baitfish schools at the surface. Fishing has depleted the trevallies and kahawai, though you may catch sight of a few small schools.

Bay of Plenty Dive Sites

The Bay of Plenty encompasses a wide swath of coast dominated by long sandy beaches. Diving centres on the offshore islands, which boast stellar visibility. Washed by the East Auckland Current, these waters host many of the spectacular marine species also found in northern NZ. The islands themselves are volcanic in origin. The only active volcano, Whakaari (White Island), and the neighboring Volkner Rocks offer some of the best diving in NZ, featuring steep pinnacles wreathed in huge schools of fish.

The region's only marine reserve lies north of Tuhua (Mayor Island), where divers find obsidian (black volcanic glass) and hot water vents. Dive boats out of Tauranga visit numerous shipwrecks, ranging from the purpose-sunk *Taioma* to the more than 100-year-old wreck of the *Taupo*.

Mount Maunganui overlooks the western bay.

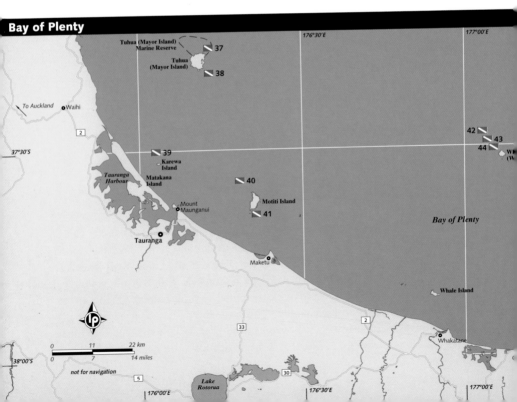

The open sandy coastline between Waihi and Whakatane is broken only by 232m (760ft) Mount Maunganui and the Maketu peninsula. From Opotiki east,

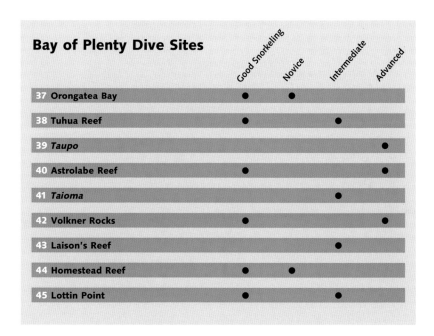

Bay of Plenty Dive Sites	Good Snorkeling	Novice	Intermediate	Advanced
37 Orongatea Bay	●	●		
38 Tuhua Reef	●		●	
39 *Taupo*				●
40 Astrolabe Reef	●			●
41 *Taioma*			●	
42 Volkner Rocks	●			●
43 Laison's Reef			●	
44 Homestead Reef	●	●		
45 Lottin Point	●		●	

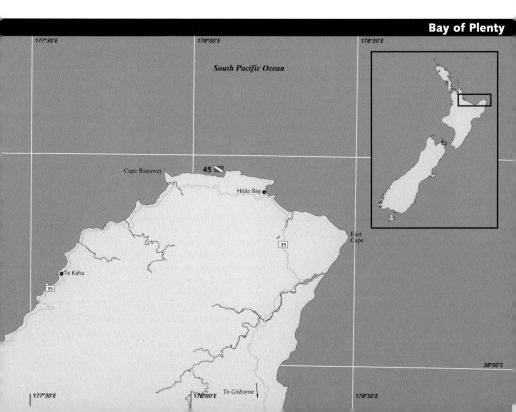

the coast features rocky reefs and pebbly beaches. Shore diving is popular between Te Kaha and Lottin Point, near the East Cape.

Most dive boats leave from Tauranga, Mount Maunganui and Whakatane, with frequent sightings of dolphins and whales. Visibility can exceed 40m (130ft) around the offshore islands but is usually 8 to 20m (25 to 65ft) along the coast. Water temperatures range between 12 and 22°C (54 and 72°F), with warmer currents off Tuhua and Whakaari.

37 Orongatea Bay

This nearshore site boasts excellent snorkeling over kelp-covered boulders. You'll see spotties, black angelfish, goatfish and scarlet and orange wrasses in the shallows. Common sea urchins cover the rocks, replaced at depth by larger black sea urchins. Though Tuhua is an extinct volcano, gas bubbles still rise from hot water vents beneath the rocks and sand.

Check beneath the boulders to find large crayfish and several moray eel

Location: NE side of Tuhua (Mayor Island)

Depth Range: Surface-20m (65ft)

Access: Boat

Expertise Rating: Novice

species, including yellow, grey, speckled and mosaic. Snappers and blue and pink maomao school atop the kelp beds. In summer kingfish pass through, breaking up the baitfish schools to feed.

The East Auckland Current bathes Mayor Island, bringing with it warm water and tropical organisms. You'll find such species as Lord Howe Island coral fish, sharpnose puffers and crimson cleaner wrasses. The latter clean blue maomao and demoiselles, sometimes aided by juvenile Sandager's wrasses. Expect to see stingrays and eagle rays amid the kelp or on the sand.

The bay offers a safe anchorage from prevailing southwesterly winds, but easterly swells can bring strong surge to the shallows. Though the Tuhua (Mayor Island) Marine Reserve was set aside in 1992, fish life has not rebounded as quickly as that in northern no-take reserves.

You might spot an eagle ray atop the kelp.

38 Tuhua Reef

Bits of obsidian, or black volcanic glass, litter the seafloor at this site, bearing witness to Tuhua's volcanic past. Lava flows formed the reef, which features steep drop-offs and large shallow flats. Scattered over the reef between 5 and 10m is wreckage from the fishing boat *San Benito*. Surge may be strong in the shallows.

Location: SE side of Tuhua (Mayor Island)

Depth Range: Surface-30m (100ft)

Access: Boat

Expertise Rating: Intermediate

The island lies in the path of the seasonal East Auckland Current, whose warm waters influence marine life. You'll find a profusion of red, green and brown seaweed. Masses of common anemones thrive in the shady spots—look amid them to spot tiger shells, triplefins and nudibranchs. Colorful firebrick sea stars are often attached to the rocks.

On any dive here you might see up to 60 species of fish. Kingfish are common, ripping through the koheru and mackerel schools. Amid the kelp are black angelfish, leatherjackets, kelpfish, marblefish, spotties, banded wrasses, porae, red moki and goatfish. Farther down among the sponges and black sea urchins you may spot mosaic, grey and yellow moray eels. Hovering above them are schools of Sandager's wrasses, demoiselles, sweeps and blue maomao.

In early summer paper nautiluses, relatives of the octopus, jet in close to the island to lay their eggs. Their fragile white shells lie scattered around the reef.

Porae and Sandager's wrasses are among the dozens of resident reef species.

39 | *Taupo*

The *Taupo* ran aground outside Tauranga Harbour in 1879 and was refloated two years later. She left in tow for Auckland, but soon began to take on water through patched holes and sank. Though her decks and superstructure have collapsed, the hull is largely intact. Take care, as the wreck is covered in trawl nets that have snagged over the years. Descend from the buoy through masses of fish, including snappers, trevallies, kingfish, tarakihi and blue maomao. Runoff from heavy rains may drop visibility on the wreck.

Blasted open to recover copper and other metals, the ship's midsection features the huge boiler and engine, which tower above the sand. Her hull is coated in sponges and other encrusting life. Large schools of butterfly perch and demoiselles hover atop the wreck, while

Location: Just north of Karewa Island

Depth Range: 30-35m (100-115ft)

Access: Boat

Expertise Rating: Advanced

golden snappers and splendid perch keep to the shadows. Check crawl spaces for big conger and moray eels and the occasional crayfish.

On the sand surrounding the wreck are goatfish, while overhead John dories stalk smaller fish. Watch your bottom time and use the mooring line for a safety stop. The wreck is wholly protected under the Historic Places Act—nothing should be taken or disturbed.

40 | Astrolabe Reef

Astrolabe Reef hosts subtropical marine life swept here by the East Auckland

Location: 8km (5 miles) NW of Motiti Island

Depth Range: Surface-37m (120ft)

Access: Boat

Expertise Rating: Advanced

Search the invertebrate growth for scorpionfish.

Current. The reeftop just breaks the surface, and Pacific Ocean swells that roll over the rock can make the shallows unpleasant. The reef drops quickly to very deep water. Wide-angle photographers will find plenty of big fish, while life on the walls will engross a macro enthusiast.

Descend through schools of demoiselles, blue maomao, sweeps, trevallies and kahawai. In summer and autumn big kingfish join the crowd, as does the occasional barracuda or tuna. Mako, bronze whaler and blue sharks also visit the reef.

A steep drop-off on the east side is covered in anemones and colorful sponges. Look among them for nudibranchs and triplefins. Large schools of kahawai and trevallies swirl behind you, while crayfish shelter within reef nooks.

Where the kelp diminishes at about 20m, the sponge gardens begin. Yellow zoanthids protrude like anemones from between black sponges. Halfbanded perch rest in the cracks beside crayfish and yellow moray eels, while butterfly perch and pink maomao school overhead. Look closely to spot scorpionfish, which glare from resting places amid the sponges, anemones and bryozoans.

41 Taioma

Upright on the sand at 28m, the *Taioma* is a WWII tugboat that was purpose-sunk as a dive site in March 2000. Descend the mooring rope near either the bow or stern and tour the ship from end to end. Already limited, visibility drops even further as divers stir up silt within the ship. Wide-angle photographers should be the first on the wreck for the best photo opportunities.

Schooling above the wreck are blue maomao, sweeps, demoiselles, small

Location: SE side of Motiti Island

Depth Range: 20-28m (65-90ft)

Access: Boat

Expertise Rating: Intermediate

snappers and tarakihi, while goatfish, leatherjackets and blue cod graze on the decks. The hull is coated in bryozoans,

Adventurous divers can enter this WWII tugboat through its upright funnel.

hydroids and stunted kelp. Look amid the anemone patches to spot blennies, triplefins and tiger shells.

The back of the boiler was removed and a series of holes were cut in the hull to allow light into the ship. You can also access the interior via the funnel. Wiring and other potential obstructions have been removed, and areas deemed unsafe have been welded shut. Still intact on the open bridge, the ship's wheel actually turns. On the afterdecks, pipes and winches from the tug's working days now serve as homes for small crayfish. More crayfish live inside the ship and venture out at night. During your safety stop, check out the goose barnacles and small fish just beneath the mooring buoys.

42 Volkner Rocks

A proposed marine reserve, Volkner Rocks is one of those ultimate open-water dives where you might see almost any pelagic species. Watch the current here, and if swells are high, drop quickly below 15m. On the east side, a rocky slope drops from 6m to a flat shelf at 18m. That's followed by a gradual slope to 30m, then a steep drop well below the sport-diving limit. The northeast wall plunges below 1,000m. Schools of massive kingfish are common, as are tuna and sharks.

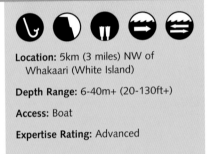

Location: 5km (3 miles) NW of Whakaari (White Island)

Depth Range: 6-40m+ (20-130ft+)

Access: Boat

Expertise Rating: Advanced

The Volkners served as a practice firing range for the NZ Air Force and Navy until 1998. The seafloor is littered with bomb

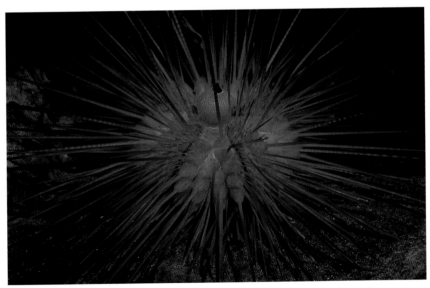

When lit by a dive light or strobe, *Diadema* sea urchins glow a striking red.

casings, and some may still be live. Do not attempt to recover any of these. Look for huge schools of golden snappers amid the kelp forest, which extends below 30m. Below the kelp are solitary corals, dead man's fingers, sponges and bryozoans.

A pinnacle known as **Diadema City** rises within 9m of the surface. Brilliant red *Diadema* urchins and firebrick sea stars cover its eastern face. Vast schools of trevallies and blue maomao are replaced by pink maomao below 20m.

Look among the rocks for such invertebrates as banded coral shrimp, Spanish lobsters and nudibranchs. Crayfish are also fairly common. Large green, or packhorse, crayfish move in around October.

43 Laison's Reef

This is another blue-water site where almost anything might swim past you in the 30m-plus visibility. From two high points the reef plunges below 150m, making buoyancy control critical. Schools of trevallies and blue maomao swirl around you in mid-water, accompanied in summer and autumn by kingfish. The reeftop is covered in kelp and hosts large resident leatherjackets and thousands of two-spot demoiselles. Watch for the striking yellow-and-black stripes of Lord Howe Island coral fish, which live amid the kelp fronds.

If a current is running, descend on the lee side of the reef. The blue maomao schools at the surface are gradually replaced by pink maomao. Look for colorful splendid perch at about 35m, just below the pink maomao. There's a good chance you'll spot blue, mako or bronze whaler sharks and perhaps an ocean sunfish, marlin or yellowfin tuna in late summer.

The walls are coated in invertebrates, and black corals are prevalent below 45m. Pause on the anchor rope for your safety stop, saving some film to photograph clouds of swirling baitfish and the kingfish that hunt them.

Location: Between Whakaari (White Island) & Volkner Rocks

Depth Range: 12-40m+ (40-130ft+)

Access: Boat

Expertise Rating: Intermediate

Schools of bright pink maomao fill the mid-water.

44 Homestead Reef

This reef lies in the shadow of the Whakaari cliffs. The surface around the boat usually boils with blue maomao and trevallies, which surround you as you descend. You'll reach the sand at 22m and meander amid the boulders. It's a great site to practice both macro and wide-angle photography.

Location: 200m (650ft) offshore, NW side of Whakaari (White Island)

Depth Range: 12-22m (40-70ft)

Access: Boat

Expertise Rating: Novice

Between the boulders are very large canyons and swim-throughs. Some walls are covered in orange soft corals and hydroids, along with encrusting, golf ball and finger sponges. Firebrick sea stars and orange ascidians add to the colorful dis-

Whakaari (White Island)

Fifty kilometers (30 miles) offshore from Whakatane, Whakaari (White Island) is NZ's most active volcano. Visible from the coast, hot water and steam continually spout from vents on the crater floor. Occasionally the island erupts, spewing ash several kilometers into the air. While the eruptions are usually short-lived, it's best to avoid the island during such an event.

Regular trips from Whakatane ferry visitors to the island by boat and helicopter. Costs include landing fees, safety equipment and a knowledgeable guide. Several charter operations accommodate divers, visiting such boulder-strewn sites as Homestead Reef.

There is no protected anchorage at Whakaari. Boats usually anchor in the lee of the island, downwind of any fallout. Take care when refilling scuba tanks close to shore. Volcanic ash can also damage dive gear left exposed on the deck.

Water visibility sometimes exceeds 40m (130ft). Large schools of fish break the surface when feeding. These are stalked by large predators such as mako, blue and bronze whaler sharks, tuna, kingfish and the occasional marlin.

play. Have a close look for nudibranchs and triplefins. Red and green crayfish extend their feelers from the cracks. The green, or packhorse, variety can be 10kg or more and are unafraid of divers.

Expect to be mobbed by fish. Schools of pink maomao, butterfly perch and blue maomao are everywhere, while tarakihi hover farther out in the blue. You'll also find red moki, bigger blue moki, marble-fish, blue cod, black angelfish, red pigfish, mados and several wrasse species. King-fish are common and will make close passes. Grey moray eels wrap themselves around long kelp strands, often where you least expect to see them.

45 Lottin Point

From the Lottin Point turnoff, the road winds down to this rocky coastline, which is diveable when swells are down. Take care when clambering over the slip-pery rocks to and from the water. The waning East Auckland Current supports diverse marine life.

Location: 10km (6 miles) west of Hicks Bay

Depth Range: Surface-30m (100ft)

Access: Boat or shore

Expertise Rating: Intermediate

Underwater, nearshore rocks are cov-ered in kelp and grazed on by urchins. Around the kelp holdfasts you'll find paua and other mollusks, including trumpets, tigers and pink opal top shells. You'll find various sponges amid the kelp, including black, small finger, golf ball and yellow encrusting species.

The terrain slopes steeply to 30m fairly close to shore, though the best diving is between 10 and 20m. Large red moki graze on the rock face beneath schools of blue maomao and kahawai. You'll also spot snappers, porae, demoiselles, butterfly perch, John dories, blue cod, dwarf scorpionfish, scarlet and Sandager's wrasses. The cracks and caves are home to yellow moray eels and the

occasional crayfish. In late summer visi-bility approaches 30m, and big kingfish visit the site.

Trumpet mollusks prey on sea urchins and sea stars.

East Coast Dive Sites

At the heart of this region are Hawke Bay (the region is known as Hawkes Bay) and the cities of Napier and Hastings. A massive earthquake in 1931 uplifted the Hawke Bay seabed, adding some 40 sq km (16 sq miles) of dry land to Napier alone. Many of the damaged buildings were restored to the style of the day, and Napier remains NZ's Art Deco capital. Side roads south of Hastings lead to rocky headlands and sandy beaches. On the southeast tip of the bay, Cape Kidnappers is home to one of the world's largest and most accessible nesting sites for gannets, which flock here between October and April.

North of Hawke Bay are the Mahia Peninsula, Poverty Bay and Gisborne, the first city in New Zealand to see the light of each new day. The rocky coastline is broken by sandy beaches and fast-flowing rivers. The Gisborne coast also boasts NZ's top surfing spots.

Diving is restricted by strong wind and swells, which, combined with runoff from erosion, limit visibility. Despite this the region offers interesting diving over varied habitats. Water temperatures range from 12 to 20°C (54 to 68°F).

The region's two marine reserves—Te Tapuwae-O-Rongokako, north of Gisborne, and Te Angiangi, south of Napier—are slowly returning to their natural state and promise good snorkeling and shallow diving. Resident marine mammals include fur and elephant seals. Just offshore is the whale migration route between Antarctica and the tropics.

Perched along Hawke Bay, Waipatiki Beach is 34km north of Napier.

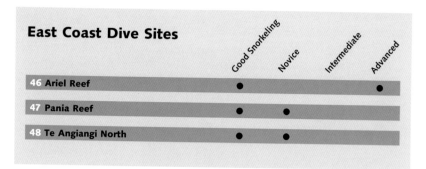

East Coast Dive Sites	Good Snorkeling	Novice	Intermediate	Advanced
46 Ariel Reef	●			●
47 Pania Reef	●	●		
48 Te Angiangi North	●	●		

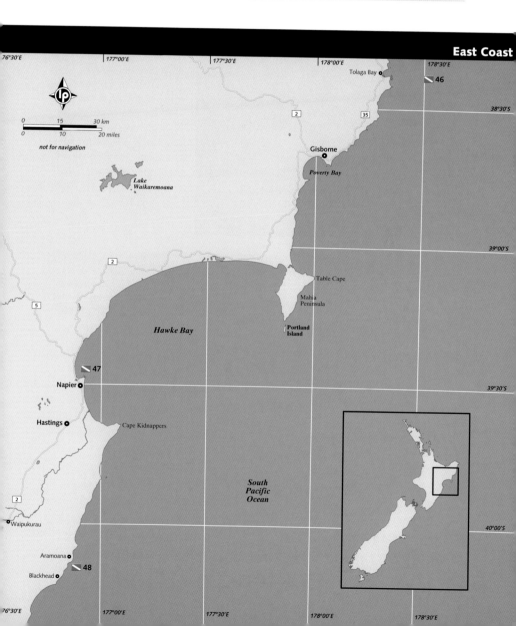

Southern Elephant Seal

Southern elephant seals are the largest pinniped species, reaching up to 6m (20ft) long and weighing more than 5,000kg (11,000 pounds). Much larger than females, males are distinguished by their inflatable snouts. When fully developed, this snout hangs over the mouth like an abbreviated elephant trunk.

These marine mammals breed on NZ's subantarctic islands. Though it's unusual to encounter an elephant seal while diving around mainland NZ, juvenile males do sometimes appear. One nicknamed Humphrey took over a boat ramp in Tauranga Harbour, returning to the Bay of Plenty over several years. Another, nicknamed Homer (see photo), ambled around the Gisborne waterfront for several months in early 2000.

46 Ariel Reef

This open-water site hosts a number of surprise visitors, including a great white shark in 2001—a thankfully rare event. You'll more likely spot blue and mako sharks. Any offshore wind or swell thwarts diving here, but the blue water makes it an appealing dive. You may encounter strong currents.

As you descend past the shallow kelp beds, watch for entangled nylon fishing line. The reef is heavily fished, and a knife is a necessity. Masses of anemones thrive between the kelp holdfasts, gradually giving way to sponges and sea tulips at depth. You'll see lots of spotties, blue moki, blue cod and banded wrasses.

Location: 10km (6 miles) east of Tolaga Bay

Depth Range: 3-30m (10-100ft)

Access: Boat

Expertise Rating: Advanced

Schools of blue moki and tarakihi mix with the occasional snapper along the reef edge. In summer large schools of kingfish move in close to feed on baitfish. Various reef crevices are home to a few conger and yellow moray eels, as well as very big crayfish.

47 Pania Reef

Large shipping buoys mark the ends of this narrow rocky reef, which runs northeast-southwest for 1.5km. Rising steeply from a muddy bottom, the reef is laced with many crevices, ledges and cracks that shelter fish and crayfish. Wait for a summer dry spell to dive here, as runoff can diminish visibility. The large swells that draw surfers to the area can make diving difficult. If a current is running, descend on the lee side of the reef.

Whatever the visibility, macrophotographers will find plenty of subjects. Amid sponges, bryozoans, hydroids and jewel anemones you'll find grazing clown nudibranchs and their orange egg masses. The reeftop is covered in mussels, seaweed and common anemones. Large spiny sea stars feed on the mussels, and blue cod will approach to nip at

Location: .5km (.3 mile) north of Napier, Hawke Bay

Depth Range: 3-20m (10-65ft)

Access: Boat

Expertise Rating: Novice

your fingers. Blennies and triplefins are everywhere.

Schools of sweeps, blue maomao and butterfly perch hover atop the reef, feeding on drifting plankton. Below them leatherjackets and red moki munch on the encrusting life, while banded wrasses and butterfish meander amid the kelp. Scour the sandy areas between rocks to find fossicking goatfish, red dahlia anemones and the occasional resting stingray. The rocks

A clown nudibranch spins a spiral of its eggs on the rocks.

themselves conceal dwarf scorpionfish and octopuses. Kingfish sometimes glide in to ambush schools of koheru, jack mackerel or kahawai.

48 Te Angiangi North

This site lies on the north end of the Te Angiangi Marine Reserve, the only marine reserve between Hawke Bay and Wellington. Rocks at the south end of Aramoana Beach are best dived in a northwesterly wind, when there's no surf. At low tide you can drive along the beach from Aramoana or Blackhead.

Swim out alongside the rocks until you reach about 6m, noting the direction of the current. Large brown kelp covers most of the rocks, with smaller red and green weeds around the holdfasts. Amid the weed you'll find large paua, sea urchins, cat's-eyes, Cook's turbans and top shells. Rocks near the sand are covered with sponges, bryozoans and sea tulips. A series of cuts between the rocks gradually drop to about 12m.

Location: 30km (19 miles) east of Waipukurau

Depth Range: Surface-12m (40ft)

Access: Boat or shore

Expertise Rating: Novice

Fish numbers have increased since the reserve was established. You'll find spotties, butterfish, banded and scarlet wrasses, kelpfish, leatherjackets, goatfish and the occasional red and blue moki. Crayfish have also increased in number and size. Avoid the rocks in strong swells.

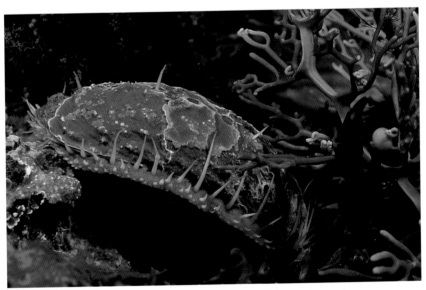

Paua, or abalone, use a muscular foot to attach to nearshore rocks.

Taranaki Dive Sites

Taranaki is on the west coast of the North Island, midway between Auckland and Wellington. It juts out into the Tasman Sea and is dominated by Mount Taranaki (Mount Egmont), a dormant volcano that rises 2,518m (8,260ft).

Sugar Loaf Islands Marine Park (Nga Motu) was established in 1986 around the eroded volcanic islets 1.5km (1 mile) offshore from Port Taranaki and Paritutu, the hill above it. The park won further protection when it was designated the Sugar Loaf Islands Marine Protected Area (SLIMPA) in 1991. Moturoa and Motumahanga are designated wildlife refuges, and landing is by permit only. NZ fur seals breed on the islands, which also host a large number of seabirds. The Taranaki coast offers world-class surfing and windsurfing, and when the winds are down, divers head out to admire the large fish schools and abundant invertebrates. As elsewhere in NZ, crayfish hunting remains popular in these waters—confirm your dive operator's focus when you book your trip.

The convergence of a northerly subtropical current and a southerly cold stream leads to a mix of northern and southern species. Water temperatures average between 12 and 20°C (54 and 68°F). Visibility can exceed 30m (100ft), though coastal rivers sometimes limit visibility to between 3 and 5m (10 and 15ft), depending on rainfall levels. The best time to dive here is in late summer, when clear blue oceanic water washes the coast and easterly winds limit swells.

The enduring image of Taranaki is the Cape Egmont light with Mount Taranaki in the distance.

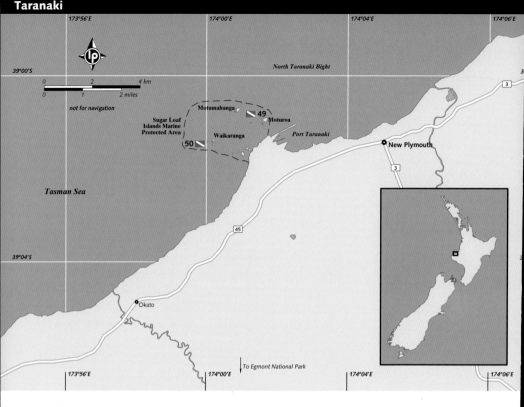

North Taranaki Bight

Tasman Sea

Taranaki Dive Sites

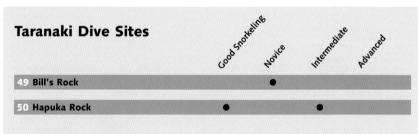

	Good Snorkeling	Novice	Intermediate	Advanced
49 Bill's Rock		●		
50 Hapuka Rock	●		●	

49 Bill's Rock

Topping out 8m below the surface, Bill's Rock is one of the volcanic spires that characterize the Sugar Loaf Islands. From the top of the pinnacle, descend the east drop-off, noting the direction of any current. Kelp grows from the many deep cuts in the rock. On the way down you'll pass a large cave filled with crayfish. Common reef fish include spotties, banded and scarlet wrasses, leatherjackets and blue cod.

Location: 300m (980ft) west of Moturoa, Sugar Loaf Islands

Depth Range: 8-20m (25-65ft)

Access: Boat

Expertise Rating: Novice

At 20m circle the base of the rock to the other side, where you may encounter snappers and tarakihi. Prolific sponge life includes black, orange and yellow encrusting and finger varieties. Closely inspect the anemones to find triplefins and mollusks.

In summer kingfish and kahawai target large schools of baitfish. Look amid the kelp on the west side to spot butterfish and red moki. The holdfasts support such interesting species as anemones, shells and hermit crabs. Resident NZ fur seals may visit you during the dive.

50 Hapuka Rock

This steep pinnacle rises from a sandy bottom at 32m to within 6m of the surface. Prevailing swells make things uncomfortable above 10m, though the effects diminish at depth. Descend on the lee side of the rock to avoid any current. There's not much kelp growth on the rocks, but schooling fish fill the reeftop, especially blue maomao. In summer kingfish will buzz you, and kahawai are also regular visitors.

Location: 400m (1,300ft) west of Waikaranga, Sugar Loaf Islands

Depth Range: 6-32m (20-110ft)

Access: Boat

Expertise Rating: Intermediate

Reef species thrive in these protected waters. Scarlet and banded wrasses, spotties, leatherjackets, blue cod, butterfly perch and red moki swirl around you, while crayfish fill the crevices. Big crayfish may emerge to check you out. A fissure splits the rock between 15 and 27m, and shafts of sunlight play through its openings on clear days. The walls are coated in sponges and hydroids, the latter concealing *Jason mirabilis* nudibranchs. Also look for clown nudibranchs, which graze on the sponges. Macrophotographers will find many tiny triplefins and camouflaged scorpionfish.

NZ fur seals may pay a visit. If you have time to play with them, they'll happily spiral around you, but if you ignore them, they'll quickly vanish.

Crayfish, or rock lobsters, lead a nomadic existence, sheltering in reef nooks between travels.

Wellington Dive Sites

There are several excellent dive sites within a 30-minute drive of downtown Wellington, NZ's capital city. Boasting a reputation as a windy city, Wellington is also known for its long, hot summers. Northerly winds shift the diving focus to the south coast, which borders the Cook Strait. Here you'll find easy shore access to the rocky reefs of Owhiro and Island Bays. Currents racing through the strait bring clear water and visibility up to 20m (65ft).

During southerly winds, the west coast affords better protection. Titahi and Pukerua Bays are accessible from shore, although visibility is often limited to 3 to 6m (10 to 20ft). Offshore sites like Kapiti Island and Hunter Bank offer better visibility and bigger fish schools, but are only diveable in calm conditions. Take care when diving offshore reefs, as strong currents are common.

Sites in Titahi Bay are accessible from shore.

Fish life is a mixture of northern and southern species. Blue cod, blue moki and tarakihi mix with red moki, kingfish and snappers offshore. Coastal sites feature prolific seaweed, which shelters juvenile fish. Macrophotographers will find ample subjects, including a variety of anemones, sea stars, paua, sponges and nudibranchs.

Average visibility is 3 to 10m (10 to 33ft) along the coast and 10 to 20m (33 to 65ft) offshore. Water temperatures range from 10 to 18°C (50 to 64°F).

Wellington Dive Sites	Good Snorkeling	Novice	Intermediate	Advanced
51 Hole-in-the-Wall	●	●		
52 Hunter Bank				●
53 North Reef	●		●	
54 The Boat Sheds	●	●		
55 Owhiro Bay	●	●		

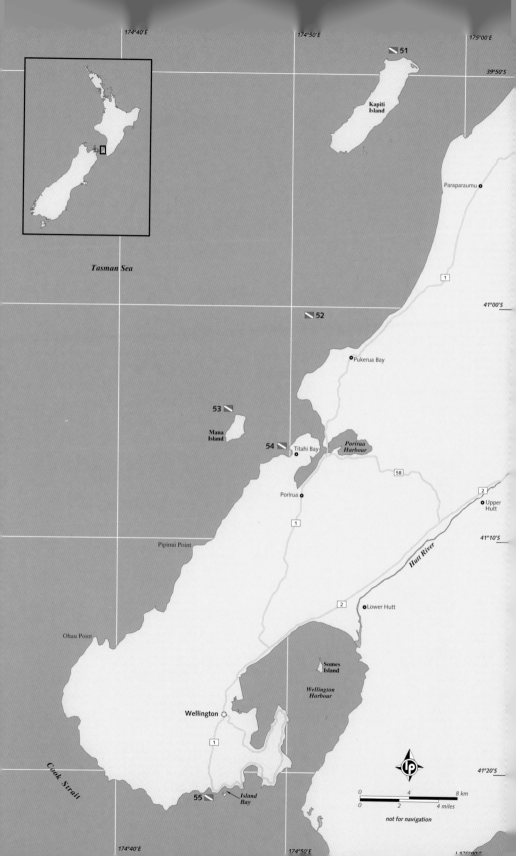

51 Hole-in-the-Wall

Kapiti Island is a nature reserve that shelters several of NZ's endangered species. Established in 1992, the Kapiti Marine Reserve extends offshore east and west of the island and offers some of the best diving in the Wellington region.

On the west side of the bay is an arch known as Hole-in-the-Wall. Topping out about 4m below the surface, the arch is wide enough to easily swim through. Take care when swells are present.

Gradually dropping to sand at 18m, the surrounding terrain features kelp-covered boulders and reefs. Silver drummers school above the kelp, scattering quickly as you approach. Spotties, blue cod and the occasional red moki graze atop the rocks. In summer kingfish are regular visitors, and snappers,

Location: Arapawaiti Point, north end of Kapiti Island

Depth Range: 4-18m (15-60ft)

Access: Boat

Expertise Rating: Novice

blue cod and stingrays stay close to the sand. Look for sea stars and anemones amid orange and yellow sponges that coat the deeper rocks. Crayfish and paua fill crawl spaces between the rocks. You may also spot octopuses, which match the color and texture of the rocks. Their close relations, broad squid, move to shallow water in summer to breed.

An octopus peers out intently from its lair beneath the kelp canopy.

52 | Hunter Bank

Due to the depth and prevailing currents, this spectacular open-water site is restricted to advanced divers. Enter during slack water and follow the anchor line to the reeftop. Every surface is coated in encrusting life, including sponges, anemones, zoanthids, hydroids and sea tulips. Check reef crevices for crayfish, as there are some very large specimens here. Conger eels often share space with the crayfish.

Location: Between Kapiti & Mana Islands

Depth Range: 18-40m+ (60-130ft+)

Access: Boat

Expertise Rating: Advanced

You'll also find New Zealand's largest nudibranch, the knobbly Wellington nudibranch, as well as the bright orange-spotted clown nudibranch. Other macro life includes sea stars and a variety of mollusks in and around the cracks in the rocks. Macro-photographers will quickly use a roll of film on these and a variety of triplefins.

Fish species vary, but on a good day you'll spot blue cod, scarlet, banded and girdled wrasses, blue moki and tarakihi. Summer visitors include kingfish and the occasional bronze whaler or blue shark. Watch your depth, as the reef edge drops away quickly. Keep track of the direction back to the anchor line so your boatman won't have to come find you.

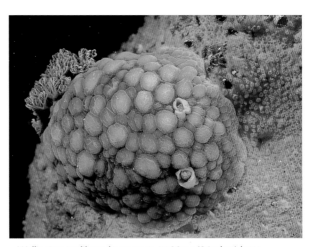

Wellington nudibranchs grow up to 20cm (8 inches) long.

53 | North Reef

The shallows here are filled with bull and giant kelp, beneath which you'll find varieties of brown, green and red seaweed. The reef drops gradually to a series of cracks and canyons. Set nets have taken their toll on fish numbers. Bring a sharp dive knife in case of entanglement.

Despite the fishing pressure, crayfish abound, usually in the deeper

Location: Mana Island, west of Porirua Harbour

Depth Range: 6-20m (20-65ft)

Access: Boat

Expertise Rating: Intermediate

cracks. Octopuses are reasonably common among the rocks and along the reef edge. Look for the stacks of shells and stones that typically surround their lairs. You'll also find blue cod, butterfish and a variety of wrasses. Macrophotographers should seek out several species of triplefins, which pose on the rocks amid the encrusting life and sea stars. Check dark recesses for common roughies and the occasional conger eel.

Below 15m, where the surge is not noticeable, there is less weed and more encrusting life, especially sponges and anemones. The odd blue moki, butterfly perch and tarakihi will swim by to inspect you, and kingfish visit in summer.

54 The Boat Sheds

Access is from Vella Street, where a rough concrete road follows the rock seawall past the boat sheds. Parking is limited, but you can unload your dive gear here and park back up the road or on the beach. Use the boat ramps for easy access to the site, where kelp borders the edge of the rocky reef. Watch for boat traffic.

Although the reef drops below 12m out in the bay, divers typically spend most time at about 6m, near the edge of the weed forests. Masses of juvenile fish

Location: North side of Titahi Bay

Depth Range: Surface-12m (40ft)

Access: Shore

Expertise Rating: Novice

live amid the weed, including butterfish, blue cod, spotties, tarakihi, banded and scarlet wrasses and the ever-present triplefins. Large paua are attached to the

Big-belly seahorses are named for their prominent brood pouches.

rocks beside the weed holdfasts, and sea stars thrive in a variety of colors and shapes. This is a great place to find sea-horses. Some wrap their tails around the weed, while others rest amid the stones and kelp debris.

55 Owhiro Bay

This popular night dive and training site is part of a proposed marine reserve. From Happy Valley Road drive west 500m along The Esplanade and park on the gravel beside the concrete boat ramp. From the ramp you'll swim southwest along the channel between the rocks. Expect some surge. Juvenile fish hover near the weed and may follow you. Large purple jellyfish, up to half a meter across, often become entangled in the kelp, where they're eaten by leatherjackets.

Location: Off south coast road, west of Island Bay

Depth Range: Surface-12m (40ft)

Access: Shore

Expertise Rating: Novice

Four shipwrecks litter the seafloor. Closest to shore is the upturned hull of the *Yung Peng*, which resembles a large rock covered in seaweed. Only the stern section remains of the broken ship. Enter it from the inshore side. Sponges, ascidians, hydroids and tunicates coat the hull. Also look for large sea stars. Resident fish here include spotties, dwarf scorpionfish, red and blue moki, marblefish, blue cod, butterfish, wrasses and red cod.

Other wreckage lies farther out. A large, heavily encrusted boiler from the *Progress* is the most prominent feature. Check inside for conger eels and small crayfish. Little remains of either the *Wellington* or the *Cyrus*, except for two anchors, a boiler, small copper pins and some copper sheathing.

Largely at the mercy of currents, jellyfish often drift into the bay.

Marlborough Dive Sites

Three main waterways comprise the Marlborough Sounds: Pelorus, Kenepuru and Queen Charlotte Sounds. As the Ice Age ended, rising seas flooded these deep valleys. You'll need a boat to access most areas, as there are many islands and otherwise inaccessible inlets and coves. Several islands are protected as bird sanctuaries—visit the Department of Conservation website (www.doc.govt.nz) for more details.

Access to the sounds is primarily by boat.

Although the sounds offer protection from wind and swells, the best diving is along the open coast. Local knowledge of tides and currents is critical, as there's a tidal range of 1.5 to 4m (5 to 13ft). Visibility averages 3 to 18m (10 to 60ft), and water temperatures vary between 10 and 18°C (50 and 64°F).

Extensive kelp forests shelter many fish species, while paua graze along the rocks amid colorful anemones, sponges and nudibranchs. Crayfish are also abundant. Divers can visit several historic

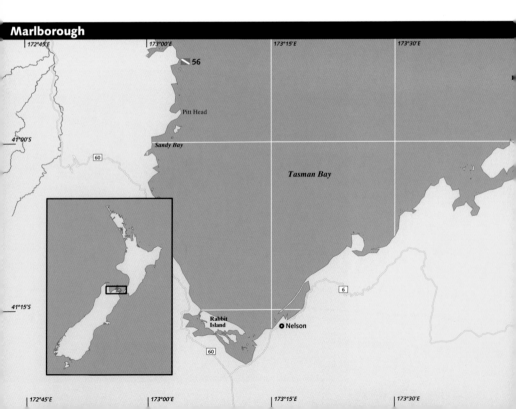

Marlborough

172°45'E 173°00'E 173°15'E 173°30'E

56

Pitt Head

41°00'S

Sandy Bay

60

Tasman Bay

Rabbit Island

6

60

● Nelson

41°15'S

172°45'E 173°00'E 173°15'E 173°30'E

shipwrecks, the oldest dating back to 1834. A more recent casualty is the Russian cruise ship *Mikhail Lermontov,* one of the world's largest diveable shipwrecks.

To the east is Nelson, one of NZ's sunniest regions. Forests, golden beaches and granite hillsides line the water's edge. Along the coast is Abel Tasman National Park, one of NZ's largest national parks and a watersports playground. Marine life has been depleted, though some species are recovering within the Tonga Island Marine Reserve. Visiting divers regularly encounter members of the island's resident seal colony.

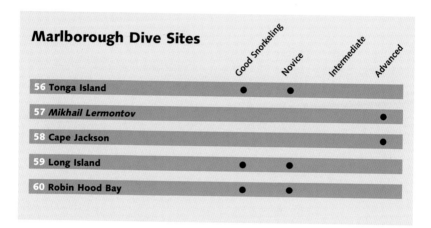

Marlborough Dive Sites	Good Snorkeling	Novice	Intermediate	Advanced
56 Tonga Island	●	●		
57 *Mikhail Lermontov*				●
58 Cape Jackson				●
59 Long Island	●	●		
60 Robin Hood Bay	●	●		

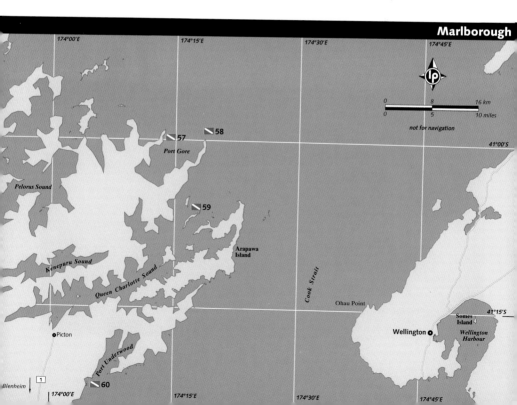

56 Tonga Island

Tonga Island lies toward the south end of the marine reserve that bears its name. Dive charters and water taxis are the best means of transport if you don't have your own boat. Visibility can exceed 12m, though it drops following heavy rains. You'll descend over rocks, seaweed and legions of sea urchins. Pink coralline algae coat the rocks and large Cook's turban shells. Typical of Tasman Bay terrain, the rocks give way to sand at 10m, which gradually slopes into the deep. Look for scallops and sea stars atop the sand.

This area has been hit hard by overfishing, and the reserve is the first step toward restocking it. The most common fish are spotties, triplefins and small schools of baitfish. Check the cracks and holes for crayfish.

Location: 1km (.6 mile) off Onetahuti Beach, Abel Tasman National Park

Depth Range: Surface-12m (40ft)

Access: Boat

Expertise Rating: Novice

Resident NZ fur seals may dive down to meet you. If you roll and play with them, they'll dart about in an impressive display of agility. It's even easier to interact with them while snorkeling. Don't attempt to climb onto the topside rocks, as seals become aggressive on land. It's possible to circumnavigate the island on a single dive.

Variable triplefins perch on their fins for a look around the rocky terrain.

Waikoropupu Springs

The country's most spectacular freshwater dive site is Waikoropupu (Pupu) Springs, on the Nelson coast near Takaka. These are the largest freshwater springs in NZ, offering some of the clearest water in the world, with up to 65m (215ft) visibility. The water is filtered over the course of several years as it wells up through limestone passages beneath the mountains. Be prepared for cold water—the temperature hovers around 11°C (52°F).

The long walk with dive gear from the car park is worth the effort. No commercial activities are permitted, and visiting divers must adhere to a code of conduct posted on signs surrounding the springs.

For an exhilarating drift dive, enter the Waikoropupu River at Fish Creek, near the car park. You'll zip downriver at up to 10km/h (6mph) in water as shallow as 30cm (1ft). Check beneath overhangs in deeper water for salmon and trout. Arrange in advance for pickup.

57 *Mikhail Lermontov*

The *Mikhail Lermontov* is a 22,000-ton, 176m passenger liner. She sank in Port Gore in February 1986 after striking rocks off Cape Jackson. Be careful when penetrating the wreck, as the ship lies on its starboard side, which can be disorienting. You should not attempt to enter any part of the ship without a knowledgeable guide. Visibility is often better inside than outside the wreck, as long as you don't disturb the silt. The ship is too large to fully explore on a single dive.

Descend the mooring line to the port side at about 15m, midway between the

Location: Port Gore

Depth Range: 13-36m (45-120ft)

Access: Boat

Expertise Rating: Advanced

bow and stern. The hull is covered with seaweed, ascidians, sponges and hydroids. Schools of tarakihi hover above spotties, blue cod, triplefins and scarlet and banded wrasses.

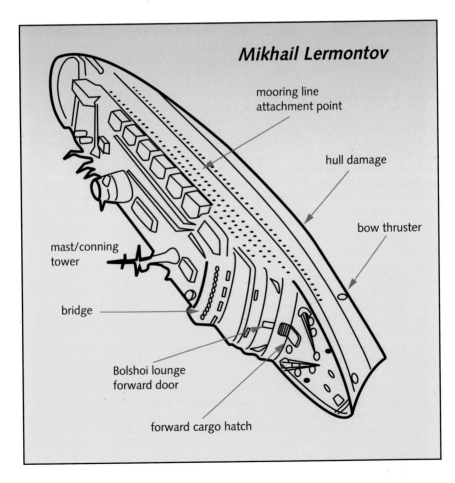

Mikhail Lermontov

mooring line attachment point

hull damage

bow thruster

mast/conning tower

bridge

Bolshoi lounge forward door

forward cargo hatch

The bridge is at 18m, and below it at 30m is the large tear in the hull. Enter the bridge to see radar, steering equipment, consoles and controls. Toward the bow you can access the ballroom, which spans the width of the ship. Bolted to the floor, tables and chairs extend from what are now the walls. A spiral staircase leads to a mezzanine and bar that overlook the dance floor—try sitting sideways on one of the barstools 25m down.

Several entrances lead to the glassed-in indoor swimming pool. Notice the signs that read NO DIVING PLEASE and CAUTION: THE POOL IS EMPTY TODAY. Two huge propellers dominate the stern, one at 27m and the other at 32m. Finish the dive where you started and use the mooring line for your safety stop.

The Sinking of a Liner

On February 16, 1986, the Russian cruise liner *Mikhail Lermontov* headed out of Queen Charlotte Sound and hit rocks as she tried to pass between Cape Jackson and Jackson Head. As the ship moved forward, she began to take on water, developing a starboard list. She was turned into Port Gore and beached, but a rising tide and offshore wind pushed the ship into deeper water, where she rests at 36m (120ft). All but one of her more than 700 passengers and crew were rescued.

58 Cape Jackson

Cape Jackson offers some of the best diving in Marlborough. Either side is diveable, depending on the weather, though heavy rains can diminish visibility. It's best to go with someone with local knowledge, as the area is prone to strong currents. Two shipwrecks lie on opposite sides of the cape. Both are more than 100 years old and are protected under the Historic Places Act.

Location: East tip of Port Gore

Depth Range: Surface-30m (100ft)

Access: Boat

Expertise Rating: Advanced

The better site is the resting-place of the ***Lastingham***, on the west side about 400m from the cape. You'll descend through schools of blue moki, tarakihi and butterfly perch. Red moki, butterfish, spotties, leatherjackets, marblefish and wrasses feed along the bottom. Distinctive circular holes in the kelp are made by butterfish. Shallow rocks are covered with masses of

Anemones cling to kelp stalks in the current.

seaweed. Look for many large paua and sea urchins.

The weeds vanish below 15m, replaced by colorful sponges, anemones and sea tulips. Peer into the deeper recesses to spot large crayfish. In summer kingfish and kahawai arrive to feed on the baitfish.

The surface often boils with fish, a spectacular site from beneath the schools.

If the west side is too rough, head for the east side and the wreck of the *Rangitoto*. Identifiable pieces of both shipwrecks lie scattered around their respective sites.

59 Long Island

A marine reserve was established around Long Island in 1993. You'll descend over a kelp forest that encompasses the shallows. Milling about above the kelp are spotties, banded wrasses, leatherjackets and butterfish. Farther down the kelp is replaced by invertebrates such as anemones, sea squirts, sponges and urchins. Inspect the hydroids to find resident *Jason mirabilis* nudibranchs.

Blue cod are becoming more common, as are butterfly perch, blue moki and tarakihi. Large kahawai schools surround divers in summer. Once you reach the sandy mud floor at 15m, be

Location: NW end of Long Island, Queen Charlotte Sound

Depth Range: Surface-15m (50ft)

Access: Boat

Expertise Rating: Novice

careful not to stir the sediment, which would ruin the visibility. Scallops, sea stars and sea cucumbers lie on the bottom. Marine reserve regulations apply—take nothing.

In the protected waters of the marine reserve, blue cod are mounting a comeback.

Check vertical cracks in the rocks for crayfish, which are increasing both in size and number. Coating the rocks are patches of large green-lipped mussels. While aboard the boat, keep an eye out for bottlenose, dusky and rare Hector's dolphins, which frequent the sound.

60 | Robin Hood Bay

Both sides of the bay promise good snorkeling and scuba diving, but the large boulders and rocky reefs to the south are favored. Kelp grows close to shore, sheltering blue moki, butterfish, banded wrasses, triplefins and spotties. Check the many crevices for crayfish, and look amid the red and green seaweed for paua, nudi-

Location: South of Port Underwood

Depth Range: Surface-15m (50ft)

Access: Boat or shore

Expertise Rating: Novice

Wholly alien in appearance, the wandering anemone crawls and drifts its way across the seafloor.

branchs and sea urchins. The best site conditions are during westerly winds following a dry spell.

As you head toward the point, the terrain gradually slopes to about 15m. The outlying rocks are covered with sea tulips and sponges, with minimal kelp growth. Macrophotographers will appreciate the variety of anemones, including wandering anemones on the kelp holdfasts, large red dahlia anemones on the sand and jewel and common anemones on the rocks. Look for seahorses and octopuses, which are well camouflaged amid the invertebrates and weeds. Seals sometimes visit the bay and may approach you for a closer look.

Canterbury Dive Sites

The Canterbury region is dominated by the Canterbury Plains, bordered by the Kaikoura Ranges and the Southern Alps. Generated by snowmelt and heavy rains, many rivers flow across the plains into the sea. While the silt they carry often clouds coastal waters, the chance to interact with marine mammals makes diving here worthwhile. Sites are centred off the Kaikoura and Banks Peninsulas. Visibility is often only 2 to 3m (6 to 10ft) but can reach 15m (50ft). Water temperatures range from 15°C (59°F) in summer to 8°C (46°F) in winter.

A small peninsula 180km (110 miles) north of Christchurch, Kaikoura lies at the convergence of two ocean currents—warm water from the north and cold water from the subantarctic. The land drops steeply into very deep water, which attracts whales and other marine mammals. Visitors can snorkel with NZ fur seals and dusky dolphins, and tour boats often encounter resident sperm whales. The rocky coastline offers good diving and is well known for an abundance of crayfish (*kai* means food and *koura* means crayfish in Maori).

Just southeast of Christchurch is the Banks Peninsula. Its numerous harbors shelter a range of wildlife. Akaroa Harbour is the longest and was the site of the first French settlement in NZ. Wildlife in the area includes Hector's dolphins, NZ fur seals and white-flippered and yellow-eyed penguins. The area's only marine reserve encompasses Flea Bay (Pohatu).

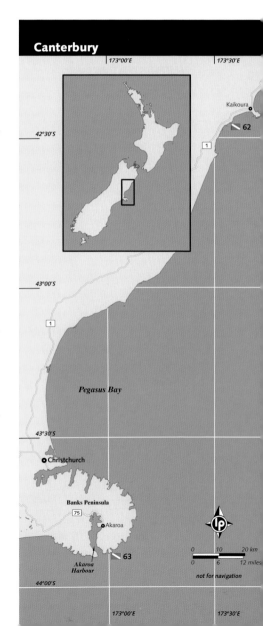

The Seaward Kaikoura Range adds a striking backdrop to all water-related activities.

Kaikoura's Marine Mammals

Kaikoura is known as the marine-mammal capital of NZ. The water a kilometer (half mile) offshore is a kilometer deep, providing ample food for the sperm whales that live here year-round. To see one of these giants sweep its tail high in the air and dive is unforgettable. Sperm whales in the Kaikoura Canyon feed mainly on groper and other deepwater fish, switching to squid when those animals migrate to the area. Once the target of coastal whalers, humpbacks and other migratory species still pass close to the peninsula. Orcas, or killer whales, are also frequent visitors.

Acrobatic dusky dolphins form pods of up to 1,000 animals and willingly interact with swimmers and snorkelers from dolphin swimming boats. Rare Hector's dolphins also live off the Kaikoura coast, but in much smaller numbers. Common and bottle-nose dolphins sometimes visit the area.

Canterbury Dive Sites

	Good Snorkeling	Novice	Intermediate	Advanced
61 Lynch's Reef	●	●		
62 Barney's Rock	●	●		
63 Flea Bay	●	●		

61 Lynch's Reef

Lynch's Reef is best dived by boat, as it's a long walk from the car park at the end of Fyffe Quay. The site features a series of reefs and deep channels around exposed rocks, which are haul-out areas for NZ fur seals.

Below the surface the rocks are covered in a mixture of kelp and seaweed atop sand between 8 and 15m. In heavy swells, descend quickly through the surge-swept shallows. You'll find bull kelp, smaller brown kelp and red and green seaweed.

Location: NE Kaikoura Peninsula

Depth Range: Surface-15m (50ft)

Access: Boat or shore

Expertise Rating: Novice

The kelp holdfasts are a mass of life, wreathed by sea stars, nudibranchs, opal top shells, sponges and sea tulips. Rock crevices hide conger eels and a few small crayfish. Also look for tiger shells and trumpet shells. Both black- and yellow-foot paua cling to the undercuts.

Red moki, sea perch, banded and scarlet wrasses, spotties and butterfish swim around the kelp. Away from the rocks tarakihi and blue moki cruise in small schools. Expect a visit from one or more of the playful NZ fur seals. On a calm day spend your surface interval snorkeling in their company.

Biscuit sea stars graze the rocks for encrusting organisms.

62 Barney's Rock

Beach access to this site is 3km past the first tunnel on State Highway 1 south of Kaikoura. Home to a breeding colony of NZ fur seals, Barney's Rock is 200m offshore. As at most shore dives on the South Island, keep your distance from the seals when entering and exiting the water.

Large strands of bull kelp swirl on the surface above smaller brown, red and

Location: 10km (6 miles) south of Kaikoura

Depth Range: Surface-18m (60ft)

Access: Boat or shore

Expertise Rating: Novice

green seaweed. Black- and yellow-foot paua cling to the rocks. You'll find spotties, banded wrasse, butterfish, sea perch, blue moki and tarakihi. The swim out is over rough terrain that drops to 8m in the sandy gutters.

The south side of the rock drops sharply to about 18m, below any surface surge. It's covered in jewel anemones from just below the kelp line. The kelp gives way to sponges, which conceal trumpet, circular saw and tiger shells. There are also plenty of sea stars, including biscuit and cushion stars, large brittle stars and giant seven-armed stars.

Crevices are home to crayfish and conger eels. Octopuses keep a low profile, as they're a favorite food for seals. The shallows from the beach out to the rock promise good snorkeling and almost guaranteed visits from the fur seals. Watch the waves on exiting.

Below the kelp line, Barney's Rock boasts a living carpet of jewel anemones

63 | Flea Bay

Access to Flea Bay is by boat or by four-wheel-drive vehicle from Akaroa. Established in 1998, it's the first marine reserve on the South Island's east coast. Though set netting and other fishing practices have depleted reef fish populations around the peninsula, fish within the reserve are rebounding. Ringed by cliffs that rise several hundred meters,

Location: Pohatu Marine Reserve, SE tip of Banks Peninsula

Depth Range: Surface-20m (65ft)

Access: Boat or shore

Expertise Rating: Novice

the bay is washed by the Southland Current. Visibility can reach 15m, though it's usually less than 10m and drops to only a few meters following southerly winds or swells.

From the beach the sandy bottom slopes gradually to rocky reefs at about 6m. Toward the mouth of the bay smaller weed gives way to bull kelp. Below the kelp, paua are recovering in numbers. Massive crayfish hide deep within volcanic cracks, while schools of big blue moki swirl around the deep reefs between 15 and 20m. Divers have recorded more than 40 reef fish species in the reserve.

Fur seals often join divers and snorkelers, and in summer Hector's dolphins frequent the bay. The surrounding cliffs are a breeding ground for white-flippered and yellow-eyed penguins, which come ashore each evening around dusk. Allow enough time to off-gas before returning to Akaroa by land, as the road climbs some 600m.

Diving with the Seals

Nearly hunted to extinction in NZ, seals are mounting a comeback. New Zealand fur seals (*Arctocephalus forsteri*) are the most common. This species ventures as far north as the Poor Knights Islands, but is more common around the South Island.

Remember that seals are wild animals and should not be closely approached on land. Keep at least 5m (15ft) away, and never get between a seal and its escape route to the sea. If they feel threatened, they can become very aggressive.

Seals are in their element underwater, where the agile animals are playful and curious, swirling in close to divers and doing barrel rolls. They'll often hover upside down, with their rear flippers pointing skyward. Always treat them with respect and be especially careful around breeding time. In a threat display, they'll approach with open jaws and veer away at the last minute. Seal-swimming excursions, which include wetsuits and snorkeling gear, run out of Kaikoura and Nelson.

Otago Dive Sites

Otago takes in a rugged piece of open rocky coast, its sandy beaches swept by the cold waters of the Southern Ocean. In calm conditions these waters offer spectacular diving beneath thick bull kelp forests. Southerly and easterly storm fronts bring diving to a halt.

Otago Harbour offers divers the only real shelter, with numerous sites and shipwrecks, many accessible from shore. Prolific marine life includes sponges, ascidians, nudibranchs and other invertebrates amid the kelp holdfasts and colorful seaweed. The long fiord-like inlet is subject to strong tidal flows and sudden weather changes. Local knowledge is essential for safe diving around the peninsula and harbor. Visibility is usually around 3m (10ft) but occasionally reaches 10m (33ft). Water temperatures range from 8 to 14°C (46 to 57°F).

Regional wildlife includes little blue penguins, yellow-eyed penguins, NZ fur seals and NZ sea lions. At the north end of the Otago Peninsula, Taiaroa Head hosts the world's only northern royal albatross colony known to live close to human habitation.

Northern royal albatross nest atop the bluffs near Taiaroa Head lighthouse.

Yellow-Eyed Penguins

Endemic to New Zealand, yellow-eyed penguins (*Megadyptes antipodes*) are among the world's rarest penguins. They range from the Cook Strait to the subantarctic islands, though only in number from the Banks Peninsula south. While farmland has replaced much of their coastal scrub and flax nesting sites, protected areas have been established at the Banks Peninsula, Oamaru, Katiki, Shag Point and the Otago Peninsula. They usually come ashore two hours before dusk, though you may spot them basking on the rocky shore during the day. They stand up to 65cm (2ft) tall and often share the beach with NZ fur seals.

Otago Dive Sites

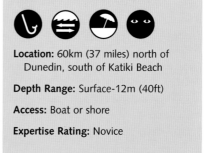

	Good Snorkeling	Novice	Intermediate	Advanced
64 Shag Point	●	●		
65 Aramoana Mole	●	●		
66 Otakou Wall				●

64 | Shag Point

Offering shelter from southerly winds, Shag Point is part of a 60-hectare wildlife sanctuary where yellow-eyed penguins and NZ fur seals come ashore. You can enter and exit along a natural rocky shelf that's exposed at low tide or via an old boat ramp, where there's less kelp and wave action. Fur seals often rest on the rocky shelf. Although playful underwater, they may be aggressive on land.

Location: 60km (37 miles) north of Dunedin, south of Katiki Beach

Depth Range: Surface-12m (40ft)

Access: Boat or shore

Expertise Rating: Novice

Don't try to swim through the bull kelp near the surface. Descend below the canopy near shore. You'll find butterfish, blue moki, blue cod, scarlet and banded wrasses, spotties and tarakihi. Wandering anemones cling to the kelp, which sways in the surge. Black-foot paua graze on algae amid the anemones. Red, brown and green seaweed thrives around the holdfasts. Biscuit and spiny sea stars are common, and scattered amid the weed are sea tulips, varying from white to reddish-orange. The rough terrain conceals lots of crayfish, some quite large. Unusual rock formations include spherical boulders similar to those found on the nearby beach.

Thick bull kelp at the surface resembles a bowl of noodles.

65 Aramoana Mole

The Aramoana Mole is a kilometer-long manmade rock wall built in 1885 as a breakwater. You can drive past a gate out onto the mole to offload your gear, then park just outside the gate. If the gate is locked, you can walk past it to the entry points or swim out from shore. Local divers have made the mole a voluntary no-take marine reserve.

A number of old hulks were sunk alongside the mole between the 1920s and '50s. About 300m from the gate is the stern post of the **Mokoia**, visible above the high-water mark. The **Poloona** is 200m farther along the mole. Fairly broken up, it bottoms out at 15m. Beside

Location: At mouth of Otago Harbour, 21km (13 miles) NE of Dunedin

Depth Range: Surface-14m (45ft)

Access: Boat or shore

Expertise Rating: Novice

it is the **Moana**, though it's difficult to discern where one stops and the other starts. The entry point for both ships is a large washout 100m from the *Paloona*'s stern, which is visible at low tide.

The wrecks are wreathed in marine growth. *Macrocystis* kelp sprouts from the rocks and wrecks and reaches the surface. Once past its floating strands, you'll find several varieties of smaller attractive weeds, ascidians and sponges. Nudibranchs munch on the ascidians, while crayfish and paua hide in the darker recesses. Beside the hulls, fields of sea tulips sway in the surge. Holes in the decks and hulls allow easy access.

Look for leatherjackets amid large schools of banded wrasses and spotties. Along the perimeter are large blue moki, tarakihi and trumpeters. The weed shelters scarlet wrasses, butterfish and rock cod.

The current can be strong and often flows against the tide at the surface. Visibility is best at high tide. The mole is a good site for night dives, but care must be taken when entering the wrecks. Experience and a good safety line are advisable. Carry a dive knife, as you may encounter fishing line in the kelp.

Wreck Etiquette

There are more than 2,000 recorded shipwrecks in New Zealand waters. Those more than 100 years old or classified as heritage sites by regional councils are wholly protected. Even if a wreck is not protected, refrain from taking souvenirs or doing any damage. Leave it as you found it for other divers to enjoy.

Several wrecks lie alongside the breakwater.

66 | Otakou Wall

Otakou Wall is a drift dive that begins or ends near beacon No. 13, depending on the tide. The dive takes about 30 minutes during slack tide, though much less time in a current. Seek local knowledge about the site and arrange a boat pickup.

Macrocystis kelp strands mark one end of the wall, 300m up the harbor from the beacon. Descend quickly to the bottom at 20m to avoid drifting away. The wall is a mass of colorful invertebrates. Sponges, ascidians, bryozoans, anemones and sea tulips cover almost every surface. Small crayfish wedge into the gaps between rocks. Also look for palm-sized decorator crabs camouflaged with sponges and ascidians. Fish life includes passing tarakihi, blue moki and large schools of spotties.

Things seem to grow bigger here, especially the sea slugs. On the grey mud between the rocks are black *Scutus* slugs,

Location: North end of Otago Harbour, near beacon No. 13

Depth Range: 8-20m (25-65ft)

Access: Boat

Expertise Rating: Advanced

or shield slugs, their white shells shaped like Roman soldiers' shields. Grazing amid the sponges and ascidians are gold-lined nudibranchs (*Chromodoris aureomarginata*) and large knobbly Wellington nudibranchs. A passing fur seal or sea lion may divert a macrophotographer's attention.

The dive ends at about 10m where the rocks peter out. Surface near the channel beacon, where the dive boat should be waiting to pick you up.

New Zealand Sea Lions

The World Conservation Union classifies endemic New Zealand sea lions (*Phocarctos hookeri*) as "vulnerable." While the total population numbers between 11,000 and 14,000, there's still concern over the number of sea lions accidentally caught and killed by squid fishermen off the Auckland Islands. All squid fishery vessels now include a sea lion excluder device on their nets, which has cut the number of fatalities. Sea lions feed on squid, barracoutas, flatfish, octopuses, jack mackerel and cod.

While sea lion bones have turned up in Maori middens in Northland, the animals virtually disappeared from the mainland more than 400 years ago. They are slowly returning from the outlying islands. There are about 100 animals along the south coast of the South Island and larger numbers at Stewart Island. They're also breeding near Catlins and on the Otago Peninsula.

Adult male sea lions have very dark coats—the dominant male often surrounded by a harem of females. Females are generally lighter, smaller and lack a mane, while young males are light brown and similar in appearance to females.

Fiordland Dive Sites

Part of a World Heritage Area on the southwest end of the South Island, Fiordland is a national park covering more than a million hectares (2.5 million acres).

Remote and wild, it's one of the least-explored areas in New Zealand. During the Ice Age, glaciers pushed through the region toward the coast, carving deep, rounded valleys. As the climate warmed, the glaciers retreated, and rising seas filled the newly formed fiords. Mountains tower more than 2,500m (8,200ft) overhead, and steep walls delve underwater below 250m (800ft).

To the north, Milford Sound is the most visited of the 14 fiords and the only one with direct road access. It's home to the Milford Sound Underwater Observatory, which offers nondivers a glimpse beneath the surface. To reach Doubtful Sound, visitors travel by boat across Lake Manapouri, then by bus over Wilmot Pass to Deep Cove at the head of the fiord. This is the setting-off point for most boat trips to Doubtful, Dusky and Breaksea Sounds.

Waterfalls cascade down sheer walls.

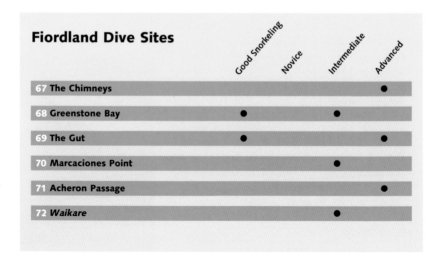

Fiordland Dive Sites	Good Snorkeling	Novice	Intermediate	Advanced
67 The Chimneys				●
68 Greenstone Bay		●	●	
69 The Gut		●		●
70 Marcaciones Point			●	
71 Acheron Passage				●
72 Waikare			●	

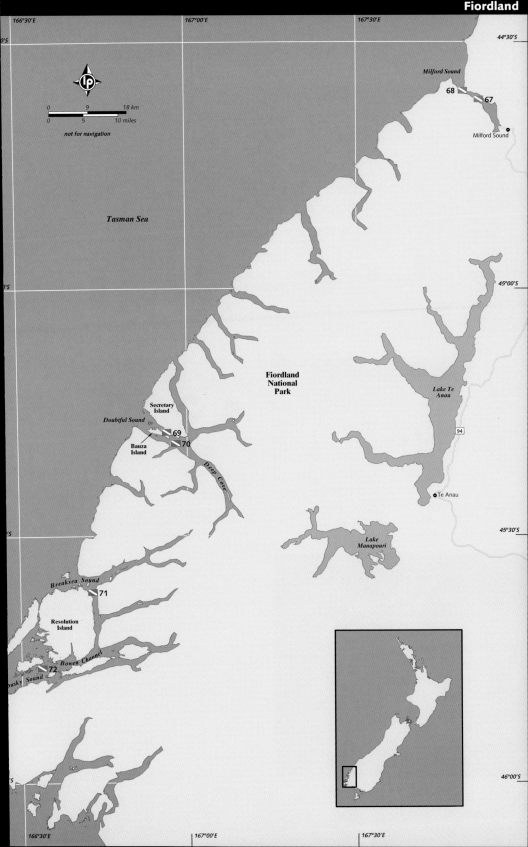

An unusual water phenomenon was first discovered in the 1970s during construction of the West Arm Power Station beside Lake Manapouri. Heavy annual rainfall (about 10m/33ft) washes tannins from rotting vegetation into the fiords, staining the surface water brown. This freshwater layer (up to 15m/50ft thick, but usually between 3 and 5m/10 and 15ft thick) rests atop the saltwater, reducing light levels and allowing shade-loving marine life to thrive in the shallows. The layers remain separate till they reach the open sea, where wind and waves break them down.

Diving is possible year-round in the sheltered upper fiords. Water temperatures below the freshwater layer vary between 10 and 18°C (50 and 64°F). Visibility can exceed 30m (100ft), and the freshwater layer often casts an emerald-green glow. Divers regularly spot resident bottlenose dolphins and NZ fur seals and also find red and black corals, sea pens and brachiopods.

Topside, Fiordland has enjoyed full protection since 1904, yet there are only two small marine reserves—Piopiotahi on the north side of Milford Sound and Te Awaatu Channel (The Gut) in Doubtful Sound.

67 The Chimneys

Within Piopiotahi Marine Reserve, this dive starts on a gently sloping rock shelf and drops down a steep wall. Good buoyancy is essential, and you should keep an eye on your depth. Protruding from the wall at 10m, a series of rock chimneys plunge to 250m. Black coral colonies grow from the wall—the live

Location: East of Dale Point, north side of Milford Sound

Depth Range: 10-25m (33-80ft)

Access: Boat

Expertise Rating: Advanced

Red corals filter the currents for food.

ones glowing white, while others host yellow zoanthid colonies. Butterfly perch and scarlet wrasses live amid the black coral, redbanded perch rest on the walls, and girdled wrasses, tarakihi and spotties mill about the chimneys.

Red corals hang from several undercuts at about 25m. Where the chimneys jut farthest into the fiord, near a large hole in the wall, are colonies of 2m black corals. From here the walls drop vertically, sporting smaller black corals. Many small crayfish extend their feelers from deep crevices.

Ascend to between 10 and 12m, where the wall is less steep and covered in green seaweed. The weed is home to a variety of biscuit and spiny sea stars, trumpet shells and several banded wrasses. Keep an eye out for small dog sharks, which will flee if you approach them. On a platform at 10m you'll find the remains of a submerged tree, as well as hydroids and grazing *Jason mirabilis* nudibranchs.

68 Greenstone Bay

This dive begins below the freshwater layer on a rocky ledge at about 7m. You'll pass large patches of blue mussels and their main predators, giant seven-armed and spiny sea stars. Tube anemones sprout from the ledge amid empty mussel shells. This is a good place to check your buoyancy before moving down the wall, which drops to about 250m. Stay above 25m and browse past colonies of 1 to 2m black corals. Look for resident

Location: South of Greenstone Point, south side of Milford Sound

Depth Range: 7-25m (25-80ft)

Access: Boat

Expertise Rating: Intermediate

snake stars, which wrap tightly around the black coral branches.

Brachiopods

Dating back more than 500 million years to the Cambrian period, brachiopods are among the earliest surviving marine species. While they may look like small bivalves, they are not related to mollusks, but comprise their own phylum. They're also known as lamp shells or ladies' toenails, and often the single top valve washes ashore and glows bright red on the tide line. Filter feeders, they form dense colonies on the shaded sides of current-swept rocks. The best places in NZ to find brachiopods are Fiordland, Stewart Island and the Leigh coast.

The wall resembles an artist's palette, daubed with multicolored sponges and ascidians. Bring a dive light to find little brachiopods in the darker recesses and red corals beneath undercuts at about 20m. Crayfish stay to the back of small caves, while feather stars protrude from reef nooks, and small hydroids grow from the walls. Large brittle stars perch on narrow ledges alongside big horse mussels, which latch on to whatever sediment they can find.

Large schools of telescope fish extend up into the freshwater layer. Small scarlet wrasses run cleaning stations, attracting tarakihi and blue moki. You'll also find schools of butterfly perch, spotties and scarlet and banded wrasses. Camouflaged against the wall are ocean perch, also known as Jock Stewarts. Solitary girdled wrasses are overly friendly and nip at divers' fingers. You may spot blue sharks and spiny dogfish.

69 The Gut

At 92 hectares, Te Awaatu Channel (The Gut) is NZ's smallest marine reserve. Start your dive at slack water, as there's often a

Location: Between Secretary & Bauza Islands, Doubtful Sound

Depth Range: Surface-40m (130ft)

Access: Boat or live-aboard

Expertise Rating: Advanced

Feather-like sea pens feed on drifting plankton.

strong current. Highlighting the site are sea pens—strange filter-feeding invertebrates that resemble quill pens of the past. Descend quickly to the sand at 35m, where the sea pens stand some 30cm high, covering the channel floor. Watch your time and head back up the wall.

Caves at the base of the wall are home to splendid perch—their reds, pinks and yellows muted at this depth. You'll also pass red corals and 1.5m black corals. Pink-and-white *Jason mirabilis* nudibranchs graze on hydroids that look like white bonsai trees.

Macrophotographers will have no shortage of subject matter in the shallows. Gold-lined nudibranchs (*Chromodoris aureomarginata*) graze amid the kelp. Look beneath the fronds for 5cm yellow sea spiders, with legs like a land spider but no body. Fish numbers have rebounded in the marine reserve, and you'll spot many big blue cod. You'll also find masses of blue mussels. Larger horse mussels (up to 40cm long) attach to very small recesses and lie quite exposed. Amid the mussels are tube anemones, their long tentacles swaying in the current.

70 | Marcaciones Point

Macrophotographers will appreciate this site. Sea stars and blue mussels dominate the shallows. Amid the empty shells perched along the ledges are tube anemones, their tentacles sweeping the gentle current. Trumpet and tiger shells graze around the kelp holdfasts.

Colonies of small, bushy black corals fringe the vertical wall. Check their branches for red, brown and yellow snake stars, as well as a few red-and-white-striped ones. Check beneath the ledges for red corals and brachiopods.

Butterfly perch and tarakihi schools swim above the kelp, while spotties and banded and scarlet wrasses hover beside the wall. Covered in pink coralline algae, circular saw shells blend into the match-

Location: SE point of Bauza Island, Doubtful Sound

Depth Range: Surface–40m (130ft)

Access: Boat or live-aboard

Expertise Rating: Intermediate

ing rocks, while mounds of empty shells mark several octopus lairs. Well-camouflaged stargazers rest on the narrow shelves—only their curved mouths and beady eyes giving them away. Glowing white sea urchins with needle-sharp spines contrast with the larger common sea urchins.

Wrapping its tentacles around black coral branches, a snake star holds position in the current.

71 Acheron Passage

This channel is approached as a drift dive due to the difficulty in anchoring (the walls are almost sheer to 300m). Currents only run about 1km/h, so you can easily stop to look at marine life or take photographs. On sunny days the black corals are silhouetted against the emerald water, the calm surface reflecting podocarp forests on the mountainside above. The sheer beauty will make you quickly forget the difficulty of reaching the site.

The freshwater layer is about 3 to 4m thick, though this varies with rainfall. Descend to about 10m to find colonies of black coral up to 3m high. Be careful not to damage their fragile branches. Inspect the lower branches and bases to spot bright yellow zoanthids, anemones, sea stars and tiger shells. Schools of butterfly perch, tarakihi and spotties all

Location: Between Breaksea Sound & Bowen Channel

Depth Range: Surface-40m+ (130ft+)

Access: Boat or live-aboard

Expertise Rating: Advanced

hang in the current or amid the black corals. Check the undercuts for brachiopods and reef nooks for crayfish.

Sea perch and blue cod sit along the wall, while striped trumpeters cruise by in small numbers. Keep an eye on the black water at the edge of visibility, where almost anything might appear. Watch your buoyancy and depth, as it's easy to stray too deep in the dim light.

72 *Waikare*

As Stop Island is close to the open coast, conditions are quite different from the inner fiord sites. Surge is a consideration, the freshwater layer is thinner and visibility is reduced.

In 1910 the 94m steamer *Waikare* struck an uncharted rock between Indian and Passage Islands and was beached on Stop Island. The passengers and crew made it safely ashore. Today the ship is a Southland District Council Heritage Site—nothing must be taken or damaged. Before it won protection, the wreck was blasted open and valuable metals were removed. She is still a good wreck dive and clearly identifiable as a ship.

The remainder of her hull looms like a wall as you approach. Schools of butterfly perch and tarakihi live on the wreck

Location: East side of Stop Island, Dusky Sound

Depth Range: 12-25m (40-80ft)

Access: Boat or live-aboard

Expertise Rating: Intermediate

alongside trumpeters, scarlet and banded wrasses and blue cod. NZ's largest nudibranch, the Wellington nudibranch, also lives amid the wreckage. This greenish-brown warty animal grows up to 20cm long. On the surrounding sand you may spot helmet and trumpet shells and scallops.

Look beneath the hull plates to find common roughies, crayfish and octopuses. Conger eels may appear on night dives. NZ fur seals make their home on Stop Island and may pass through or stop and play during your dive.

Black Coral

In Fiordland alone there are an estimated 7 million colonies of black coral (*Antipathes fiordensis*). Each treelike colony is composed of bushy white polyps that cover a black skeleton. This hard skeleton is used to make jewelry in some countries, although black corals are absolutely protected under NZ's Wildlife Act.

Usually found in depths greater than 40m (130ft), the black corals in Fiordland live at less than 10m (33ft). They grow perpendicular to the fiord walls, reaching up to 4m (13ft) in height. Some are hundreds of years old.

Black corals live in symbiosis with snake stars, which wrap tightly around their branches during the day, unraveling at night to feed on debris from the surface of the corals. The colonies also host sponges, zoanthids, mollusks and anemones. Butterfly perch and scarlet wrasses often hover amid the branches and sometimes wedge themselves in at night for protection.

Stewart Island (Rakiura) Dive Sites

New Zealand's third-largest island, Stewart Island is 64km (40 miles) long and 40km (25 miles) wide, with only about 20km (12 miles) of roads. Its Maori name, Rakiura, means "glowing skies," perhaps referring to the dramatic blood-red sunsets or to the aurora australis, or southern lights, often seen in the southern sky. The island lies 21km (13 miles) south of the South Island. Access is by a 60-minute ferry trip or a 15-minute flight.

About 85% of the island is national parkland, home to several endemic species of flora and fauna. The climate on the island is milder than many South Island regions. Temperatures average 10 to 17°C (50 to 63°F).

In addition to tourism, the sea contributes to the island's economy. Commercial fishers take paua (abalone), crayfish, blue cod and oysters. Salmon and mussel farms have sprung up, and paua farming is under consideration.

Paterson Inlet comprises 100 sq km (40 sq miles) of sheltered waterways and numerous bush-clad islands. At the centre of the inlet is Ulva Island, a longtime

Another spectacular sunset over Oban, Stewart Island's principal settlement.

132

sanctuary for endangered birds. Near its mouth is Oban, Stewart Island's main town. A proposed marine reserve would protect part of Paterson Inlet, though commercial fishers voluntarily don't fish, dredge for shellfish or use set nets in the inlet. Charter boat operators also limit their take of fish and crayfish.

The marine life is spectacular, with schooling fish amid towering kelp forests. Beneath the kelp canopy you'll find seahorses, sea tulips, sponges, nudibranchs, anemones, paua and colorful sea stars. A subtropical current from the Tasman Sea protects the island from the cooler subantarctic water. Water temperatures average 8 to 14°C (46 to 57°F), and visibility ranges from 10 to 20m (33 to 65ft).

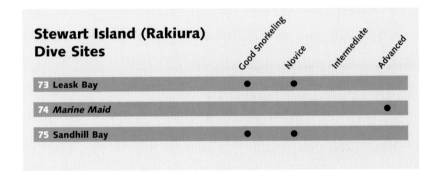

Stewart Island (Rakiura) Dive Sites	Good Snorkeling	Novice	Intermediate	Advanced
73 Leask Bay	●	●		
74 Marine Maid				●
75 Sandhill Bay	●	●		

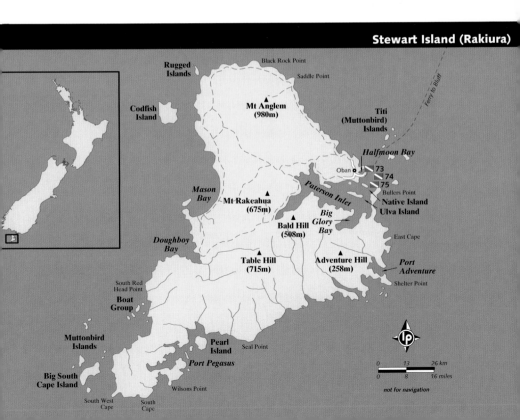

Paua

New Zealand is home to three species and one subspecies of paua, or abalone. The most common is the black-foot paua (*Haliotis iris*), which feeds by scraping algae from rocks with

an appendage called a radula. In northern waters the shells grow rapidly but remain relatively thin and small (less than 90mm), making them unsuitable for jewelry. In colder waters—especially the Cook Strait, Kaikoura, Fiordland and Stewart Island—they grow slower and thicker.

NZ paua shells flaunt deep blues and rich greens with flashes of pink and yellow. It's thought that the color varies by region and the type of algae on which the paua graze. The animals have been commercially harvested since the early 1950s, and a paua pearl industry has recently developed. Harvesters used to dump the paua meat at sea, though demand for the meat has boomed in recent years. The Maori value it as a food source, and Maori artists use the shells as eyes in their figure carvings.

Paua cannot be taken while using or in possession of any underwater breathing equipment. Black-foot paua must measure at least 125mm in length, and the maximum take per day per person is 10.

73 Leask Bay

Gear up at the ramps in front of the boat sheds, then head to the east side of the beach, a short walk from the road. As you swim over the sand toward the east point, you'll spot sea stars, sea hares and volute shells. The most interesting area is where the sand meets the rocks. Blue cod and spotties will likely follow you.

Kelp begins at about 6m and reaches the surface. Among the holdfasts you'll find wandering and pink-tipped anemones, seahorses, pipefish, sea tulips and many more sea stars. Paua cling to the

Location: South side of Halfmoon Bay, just east of Oban

Depth Range: 4-10m (13-33ft)

Access: Shore

Expertise Rating: Novice

rocks at the edge of the kelp amid colorful sponges, common anemones and ascidians. Several triplefin species perch on the rocks and kelp, making excellent macro subjects. Banded and scarlet wrasses abound here.

The sandy seafloor reaches 10m at the point and slopes gradually away. Look for small schools of tarakihi and blue moki. Also keep an eye out for southern pigfish, which use broken kelp fronds as cover.

Fur seals and the occasional NZ sea lion may seek you out during the dive. Usually playful, they may also engage in threat displays, approaching from the front with bared teeth and possibly mouthing your fins. They usually tire of this after several passes and disappear.

74 *Marine Maid*

The *Marine Maid* is a 20m cargo vessel that sank after hitting the Barclay Rocks in March 2000. Currents often sweep the wreck, so it's best to jump in near the mooring buoy and follow the rope down.

The first signs of life are sea tulips and other invertebrate growth on the rope. At about 20m you'll discern the outline of the ship, which sits upright on the sand. Depth on deck is 30m, dropping to 35m on the sand. Watch your bottom time.

Resident fish include blue moki, spotties, leatherjackets and wrasses. Inquisitive blue cod may nip at your fingers. Sponges

Location: Off Barclay Rocks, near entrance to Halfmoon Bay

Depth Range: 30-35m (100-115ft)

Access: Boat

Expertise Rating: Advanced

and ascidians are slowly covering the wreck, and sea tulips bend in the current. Sea perch blend in amid the growth on deck, and oblique swimming blennies

Sea tulips are stalked, filter-feeding animals whose color comes from encrusting sponges.

school overhead. Triplefins are common and unafraid of divers.

The machinery on deck looks as though it might still work—the chains attached to anchors and the motors coated lightly in sand. Thousands of current-borne oyster shells have collected atop the sand around the ship. Ascend via the mooring rope and make your safety stop amid the sea tulips.

75 Sandhill Bay

A boat dive is the best option here. Alternatively, a water taxi from Golden Bay can drop you on the beach at Sandhill Bay and return for a prearranged pickup.

Location: NE side of Native Island, Paterson Inlet

Depth Range: 6-12m (20-40ft)

Access: Boat or shore

Expertise Rating: Novice

The kelp forests shelter numerous species.

The best diving is amid the *Macrocystis* kelp forests, which begin at 6m on the rocky reef and peter out at 12m. The forests are home to scarlet, banded and girdled wrasses, blue cod, blue moki, trumpeters and spotties.

Very large black-foot paua attach to rocks in the shallows, while smaller yellow-foot paua keep to rocks at the outer edge of the kelp. Large red brittle stars crawl across the sand amid circular saw shells.

You'll find lots of activity in the transition zone between the sand and the kelp holdfasts on the rocks. You won't be alone, as masses of blue cod (from juveniles to large dark adults) will follow you. The fish with the glowing green eyes that hover a foot or so from your mask are girdled wrasses. Small crayfish hide in the crevices, often surrounded by ascidians, sponges and anemones.

Marine Life

Swept from the north by the subtropical East Auckland Current and from the south by the icy Southern Ocean, New Zealand's coastline supports a great diversity of marine species. Some species are found throughout the region, while others are restricted to local waters. Other areas boast a mix of temperate and cold-water species. Divers may also encounter playful fur seals, sea lions and dolphins.

Though it would be impractical to list all the species you are likely to see while diving in NZ, this section will identify some of the more common vertebrates and invertebrates. The next section describes potentially harmful or dangerous marine life you might encounter.

Keep in mind that both English and Maori names are used freely by divers and are often inconsistent. The two-part scientific name is more precise. This system is known as binomial nomenclature—the method of using two words (shown in italics) to identify an organism. The first italic word is the genus, into which members of similar species are grouped. The second word, the species, refers to a recognizable group within a genus whose members are capable of interbreeding. Where the species is unknown or not yet named, the genus name is followed by *sp.*

Common Vertebrates

lizardfish
Synodus doaki

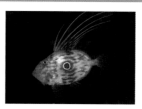

John dory
Zeus faber

big-belly seahorse
Hippocampus abdominalis

marblefish
Aplodactylus arctidens

toadstool groper
Trachypoma macracanthus

blue moki
Latridopsis ciliaris

red moki
Goniistius spectabilis

redbanded perch
Hypoplectrodes huntii

snapper
Pagrus auratus

goatfish
Upeneichthys lineatus

spotty
Notolabrus celidotus

Lord Howe Island coral fish
Amphichaetodon howensis

demoiselle
Chromis dispilus

red pigfish
Bodianus unimaculatus

scarlet wrasse
Pseudolabrus miles

blue cod
Parapercis colias

kahawai
Arripis trutta

blue-eyed triplefin
Notoclinops segmentatus

crested blenny
Parablennius laticlavius

leatherjacket
Parika scaber

clown toado
Canthigaster callisterna

Common Invertebrates

golf ball sponge
Tethya ingalli

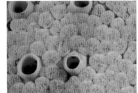

yellow boring sponge
Cliona celata

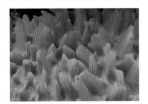

encrusting sponge
Polymastia granulosa

dead man's fingers
Alcyonium aurantiacum

common anemone
Actinothoe albocincta

wandering anemone
Phlyctenactis tuberculosa

zoanthids
Parazoanthus sp.

solitary coral
Monomyces rubrum

royal helmet shell
Semicassis royana

aeolid nudibranch
Jason mirabilis

clown nudibranch
Ceratosoma amoena

biscuit sea star
Pentagonaster pulchellus

eleven-armed sea star
Coscinasterias calamaria

red rock crab
Plagusia chabrus

red crayfish (rock lobster)
Jasus edwardsii

Hazardous Marine Life

Marine animals almost never attack divers, but many have defensive and offensive weaponry that can be triggered if they feel threatened or annoyed. The ability to recognize hazardous creatures is a valuable asset in avoiding injury. Following are some of the potentially hazardous species found in New Zealand.

Shark

Sharks come in many shapes and sizes in NZ. Divers most often spot bronze whaler, blue, mako, sand, seven-gill and hammerhead sharks. The white pointer (or great white) shark is a rare visitor, usually attracting media coverage far above its newsworthiness. They are drawn to seal and sea lion colonies around breeding times, especially at the Chatham and subantarctic islands. While most species are shy, such as the pictured carpet shark, there are occasional attacks. Avoid spearfishing or carrying fish bait and your likelihood of being attacked will greatly diminish. Face and quietly watch any shark that is acting aggressively and be prepared to push it away with your camera, knife or tank. If a shark does bite a fellow diver, stop the bleeding, reassure the patient, treat for shock and send for immediate medical help.

Moray Eel

Distinguished by their long, thick, snakelike bodies and tapered heads, moray eels come in a variety of colors and patterns. Don't feed them or put your hand in a dark hole—eels have the unfortunate combination of sharp teeth and poor eyesight and will bite if they feel threatened. If you are bitten, don't try to pull your hand away suddenly—the teeth slant backward and are extraordinarily sharp. Let the eel release your hand and then surface slowly. Treat with antiseptics, anti-tetanus and antibiotics. Moray eels are found north of Hawke Bay, while conger eels are more common in the south.

Stingray

Stingrays and eagle rays are common in northern NZ, but rarely found south of the Cook Strait. They often rest partially buried in the sand and are harmless unless you sit or step on them. Shuffle your feet when entering shallow water where rays may be present and do not corner them. If a ray feels threatened, it may lift its wings and tail in a threat display. The stingray has one or two

venomous barbs at the base of its tail. These barbs can easily pierce a wetsuit. Immerse a wound in nonscalding hot water for 30 to 90 minutes and seek medical attention. In the case of an open wound, stop the bleeding, treat the patient for shock and send for immediate medical help.

Scorpionfish

Scorpionfish are well-camouflaged creatures that have poisonous spines along

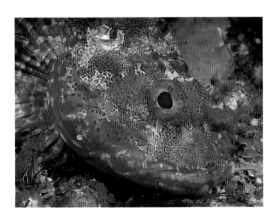

their dorsal fins. They are often difficult to spot, since they typically rest quietly on the bottom, looking more like rocks. Practice good buoyancy control and watch where you put your hands. Scorpionfish wounds can be excruciating. To treat a puncture, wash the wound and immerse it in nonscalding hot water for 30 to 90 minutes. Administer pain medication if necessary.

Jellyfish

Jellyfish injure by releasing stinging cells contained in their trailing tentacles.

Stings are often just irritating, not painful, but should be treated immediately with vinegar. As a rule, the longer the jellyfish tentacles, the more painful the sting. They are common along the NZ coast in spring and early summer. A far greater problem is the Portuguese man-of-war, also called the blue bottle (see photo). This

distant cousin of the jellyfish floats at the surface, with a distinctive blue air sac and very long trailing tentacles. Blue bottles often wash ashore in large numbers after prolonged northerly or easterly winds. Even those that look dead can still inflict a severe sting. Sting symptoms range from a mild itch to intense pain, blistering, skin discoloration, shock, breathing difficulties and even unconsciousness. Remove the tentacles—preferably with tweezers, though anything but bare hands will do. Apply a decontaminant such as vinegar or diluted ammonia and seek immediate medical aid. Allergic reactions can be severe and life-threatening.

Sea Urchin

NZ has many varieties of sea urchins. They vary in coloration and size, from the short sharp spines of shallow-water common sea urchins to the long needle-sharp spines of the deepwater varieties. The spines can easily penetrate neoprene wetsuits, booties and gloves. Treat minor punctures by extracting the spines and immersing the wound in nonscalding hot water. More serious injuries require medical attention.

Kelp

Though not inherently dangerous, kelp presents an obstacle to divers, who can become entangled in the plant. Common on the east coast of northern NZ, *Ecklonia* and *Lessonia* kelp strands are easily shed, but the longer *Macrocystis* and *Durvillea* species, found in cooler waters, are much tougher to break. When diving beneath a kelp bed, move slowly and be aware of your surroundings. Search for an opening in the canopy before surfacing. If you do become entangled, don't panic or thrash around. Either wait for your buddy to remove the problem strands or calmly snap or cut the strands with a knife yourself. Also watch for fishing line, which often tangles in kelp, and use caution when returning to shore over slippery kelp-covered rocks.

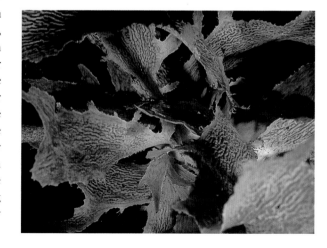

Diving Conservation & Awareness

Commercial and recreational fishing place immense pressure on New Zealand's marine environment. There are restrictions on the size and numbers of certain fish and shellfish species that can be taken, but poachers have targeted paua (abalone) for the high price it fetches on the black market. While no-take marine reserves allow fish to recover in some areas, the reserves only protect about 1% of NZ's coastal waters. Obstacles to proposed reserves include funding shortfalls and commercial opposition.

One success story comes from the Cape Rodney–Okakari Point (Goat Island) Marine Reserve, NZ's first marine reserve. Prior to formation of the reserve in 1975, resident fish and crayfish populations were in serious decline, allowing sea urchins to thrive and ravage the kelp. Recovering fish and crayfish have since kept the sea urchins in check, allowing the kelp forests to replenish and offer shelter to more species.

A network of similar reserves covering every type of marine habitat would help to reestablish sustainable populations of fish and marine life. The NZ government has pledged to protect 10% of the country's coastal waters by 2010.

Marine Reserves & Regulations

Regulations protect all plant and animal life within marine reserve boundaries. Fishing is prohibited, and nothing may be removed or introduced. The Department of Conservation (www.doc.govt.nz) manages the reserves, and regional DoC offices provide informational pamphlets showing reserve boundaries and describing resident marine life.

Outside of the reserves, local regional councils administer several marine parks, with varying regulations. For example, the Tawharanui Marine Park, north of Auckland, is a no-take zone, while the Sugar Loaf Islands Marine Protected Area, near New Plymouth, and the Mimiwhangata Marine Park, in Northland, allow some fishing. These parks may eventually be designated marine reserves.

Marine areas of traditional importance to Maori are protected under the Fisheries Act as *taiapure* and *mataitai* reserves. Local Maori committees can recommend regulations for fishery management within taiapure reserves, while mataitai reserves are managed directly by the local committees, which can restrict or prohibit non-commercial fishing activities.

The Wildlife Act protects all native species of black coral, red coral and spotted black gropers throughout NZ waters, but visiting species such as Queensland gropers are unprotected outside marine reserve boundaries. NZ should mirror other Pacific nations and grant such species umbrella protection.

You don't need a saltwater fishing license, but there are regional harvest limits regarding species, sizes and numbers. Take only what you need, and return any undersized fish. There are also restrictions on acceptable shellfish sizes and numbers, as well as seasonal closures. Paua and mussels cannot be taken while using, or in possession of, underwater breathing equipment. Crayfish (rock lobsters) must meet size limits and cannot be taken if bearing eggs or when their shells are soft. Check specific regulations with the Ministry of Fisheries (www.fish.govt.nz).

Confirm regulations with the Ministry of Fisheries before taking any crayfish (rock lobsters).

Marine Mammal Regulations

Whales, dolphins, seals and sea lions all fall under the Marine Mammal Protection Act. Boats should approach whales from the side or from behind and may not come within 50m (165ft). Swimming with whales is also prohibited.

Dolphins often approach boats and bow ride, but swimming with them is only permitted if your charter boat operator has the proper license. Don't swim with them while they are feeding or resting. Refrain from chasing dolphins if they show no interest, and avoid touching them, as their skin is delicate.

Do not come within 5m (15ft) of seals and sea lions on land, as they can be aggressive. Underwater, they're acrobatic and can be quite playful.

New Zealand fur seals can be aggressively territorial, especially during summer breeding season.

Responsible Diving

Dive sites are often along reefs and walls covered in prolific marine life. It only takes a moment—an inadvertently placed hand or knee, or a careless brush or kick with a fin—to destroy this fragile, living part of our delicate ecosystem. By following certain basic guidelines while diving, you can help preserve the ecology and beauty of the reefs.

1. Never drop boat anchors onto a reef. Encourage dive operators and regulatory bodies in their efforts to establish permanent moorings at appropriate dive sites.

2. Practice and maintain proper buoyancy control and avoid over-weighting. Be aware that buoyancy can change over the period of an extended trip. Initially you may breathe harder and need more weighting; a few days later you may breathe more easily and need less weight. Tip: Shift your weight belt and tank to maintain a horizontal position—raise them to elevate your

See Any Seahorses?

Seahorse numbers in NZ waters have declined in recent years. The reasons are unclear, so researchers have established a survey to gather data and ultimately seek full legal protection for seahorses. To report any seahorse sightings in NZ, please contact the researchers at:

Survey Seahorse 2000
P.O. Box 20-296
Glen Eden
Auckland, New Zealand 1230
☎ 09-827 7008
seahorse2000@xtra.co.nz

feet, lower them to elevate your upper body. Also be careful about buoyancy loss: As you go deeper, your wetsuit compresses, as does the air in your BC.

3. Avoid touching living marine organisms with your body and equipment. Choose handholds carefully to avoid harming marine life.

4. Take great care in underwater caves, archways and ledges. Diving in such tight spaces is especially dangerous during heavy surge. Take turns inspecting the interiors of caves and ledges to lessen the danger.

5. Secure gauges, computer consoles and the octopus regulator so they're not dangling—they're like miniature wrecking balls to a reef and can become entangled in kelp.

6. When swimming in strong currents, be extra careful about leg kicks and handholds.

7. Photographers should take extra precautions, as cameras and equipment affect buoyancy. Changing f-stops, framing a subject and maintaining position for a photo often conspire to thwart the ideal "no-touch" approach. When you must use holdfasts, choose them intelligently.

8. Resist the temptation to collect or buy marine life souvenirs. Aside from the ecological damage, collection of marine souvenirs depletes the beauty of a site and spoils other divers' enjoyment. The same goes for marine archaeological sites (mainly shipwrecks). Respect their integrity. Some sites are protected from looting by law.

9. Ensure that you take home all your rubbish. Plastics in particular pose a serious threat to marine life.

10. Resist the temptation to feed fish. You may disturb their normal eating habits, encourage aggressive behavior or feed them food that is detrimental to their health.

11. Minimize your disturbance of marine animals. Regulations govern how closely you may approach whales, dolphins and seals.

Marine Conservation Organizations

Reefs and oceans face unprecedented environmental pressures. The following groups are actively involved in promoting responsible diving practices, publicizing environmental marine threats and lobbying for better policies:

Cousteau Society
cousteau@cousteausociety.org
www.cousteausociety.org

Greenpeace New Zealand
☎ 0800-223 343
www.greenpeace.org.nz

Ocean Futures
www.oceanfutures.com
contact@oceanfutures.com

Project Aware Foundation
www.padi.com/aware
aware@padi.com

Project Jonah
☎ 09-302 3106
orca@ezysurf.co.nz

Whale & Dolphin Adoption Project
www.adopt-a-dolphin.com
info@adopt-a-dolphin.com

Listings

Telephone Calls

If you are calling within New Zealand, dial 0 + the area code + the local 7-digit number. Toll-free numbers within NZ are preceded by 0800 or 0508. Mobile phone numbers are preceded by 021, 025, 027 or 029.

To call NZ from overseas, dial the international access code for the country you are calling from (in the U.S. it's 011) + 64 (NZ's country code) + the area code + the 7-digit local number.

Diving Services

Dive centres throughout NZ offer a range of classes, from resort courses to specialty and instructor training. Certification agencies include PADI, SSI and NAUI. You'll also find plenty of airfill stations.

Services include guided diving and snorkeling trips, dolphin and seal swimming, pleasure cruises, watersports, fishing, underwater scooter rentals and underwater camera rental. Some dive centres provide their own boats, while others make arrangements through independent operators.

Northland & Poor Knights Islands

A to Z Diving
13-15 Whatuwhiwhi Road, Whatuwhiwhi
☎/fax: 09-408 7077
www.atozdiving.co.nz
andre@atozdiving.co.nz
Dive Shop: yes **Rentals:** yes
Air: yes **Courses:** yes
Boat: *Rock Hopper* (6m, 6 divers)
Trips: Karikari Peninsula, *Rainbow Warrior*, Cavalli Islands

Bay Dive & Fishing Tackle
41 Kerikeri Road, Kerikeri
☎ 09-407 5585 fax: 09-407 5591
www.diveandfish.co.nz
baydive@diveandfish.co.nz
Dive Shop: yes **Rentals:** yes
Air: yes **Courses:** yes
Boat: *Mini* (5.6m, 5 divers)
Trips: Bay of Islands, *Rainbow Warrior*

Coopers Beach Sports
172 State Highway 10, Mangonui
☎/fax: 09-406 0592
www.doubtlessbay.co.nz
info@doubtlessbay.co.nz
Dive Shop: yes **Rentals:** yes
Air: yes **Courses:** yes
Boat: *Sinbad* (5.4m, 6 divers)
Trips: Doubtless Bay, *Rainbow Warrior*

Dive HQ Whangarei
41 Clyde St., Whangarei
☎ 09-438 1075 fax: 09-430 0854
www.divenow.co.nz
sub.aqua.dive@clear.net.nz
Dive Shop: yes **Rentals:** yes
Air: yes; nitrox available **Courses:** yes

Dive North Bay of Islands
Paihia Wharf, Paihia
☎ 09-402 7079 fax: 09-402 7136
www.bay-of-islands.co.nz/diving/divenorth.html
divenorth@xtra.co.nz
Dive Shop: no **Rentals:** yes
Air: yes **Courses:** yes
Boat: *Lady Gail*, (7.4m, 7 divers)
Trips: *Rainbow Warrior*, Bay of Islands

Dive Poor Knights
57 Motel Road, Tutukaka
☎/fax: 09-434 3828
toll-free ☎ 0800-564 448
www.nzdive.com
knights@nzdive.com
Dive Shop: no **Rentals:** yes
Air: yes **Courses:** no
Boat: *Crayzee Diver* (11.2m, 10 divers)
Trips: Poor Knights Islands, Tutukaka

Northland & Poor Knights Islands (continued)

Dive! Tutukaka & Poor Knights Dive Centre
Marina Road, Tutukaka
☎ 09-434 3867 fax: 09-434 3884
toll-free ☎ 0800-288 882
www.diving.co.nz
info@diving.co.nz
Dive Shop: yes **Rentals:** yes
Air: yes **Courses:** yes
Boats: *El Tigre* (17m, 16 divers), *Bright Arrow*
(11m, 14 divers), *Hendrik J* (11m, 16 divers),
Arrow (10m, 12 divers)
Trips: Poor Knights Islands, Tutukaka
Other: Dolphin swimming, whale watching,
kayaking

Dolphin Discoveries, Paihia
corner of Marsden & Williams Roads
Paihia
☎ 09-402 8234 fax: 09-402 6051
toll-free ☎ 0800-365 744
www.dolphinz.co.nz
dolphin@igrin.co.nz

Dolphin Rendezvous
Doubtless Bay Information Centre, Mangonui
☎ 09-406 0914 fax: 09-406 0912
www.paradisenz.co.nz
clypsofishing@actrix.co.nz

Fullers Bay of Islands
81 Marsden Road, Paihia Wharf, Paihia
☎ 09-402 7421 fax: 09-402 7831
toll-free ☎ 0800-653 339
www.fullers-bay-of-islands.co.nz
reservations@fullers-bay-of-islands.co.nz
Other: Dolphin swimming

Knight Diver Tours
30 Whangarei Heads Road, Whangarei
☎ 09-436 2584 fax: 09-436 2758
toll-free ☎ 0800-766 756
www.poorknights.co.nz
knightdiver@poorknights.co.nz
Dive Shop: no **Rentals:** yes
Air: yes **Courses:** yes
Boat: *Knightdiver* (11m, 15 divers)
Trips: Poor Knights Islands

Matauri Kat Charters
Matauri Bay Holiday Park
☎ 09-405 0525 or 025-244 1319
toll-free ☎ 0800-492 774
www.warrior1.com
garygillbanks@hotmail.com
Dive Shop: no **Rentals:** yes
Air: yes **Courses:** no
Boat: *Matauri Kat* (5.1m, 4 divers)
Trips: *Rainbow Warrior*, Cavalli Islands

Norseman Dive Charters
71 Motel Road, Tutukaka
☎/fax: 09-434 3605
phil@nzwide.com

Dive Shop: no **Rentals:** no
Air: yes **Courses:** no
Boat: *Norseman* (13m; 10 divers daytrips, 6
divers live-aboard)
Trips: Poor Knights Islands, Northland coast

Octopus Divers
16 Reinga Road, Kerikeri
☎/fax: 09-407 4900
octopusdivers-nz.com
octopus@xtra.co.nz
Dive Shop: no **Rentals:** yes
Air: no **Courses:** yes
Boat: *Octopus 1* (5.7m, 4 divers)
Trips: *Rainbow Warrior*, Cavalli Islands, Bay of
Islands

Pacific Hideaway Charters
13 Moody Ave., Whangarei
☎ 09-437 3632 fax: 09-437 2469
toll-free ☎ 0800-693 483
www.divenz.co.nz
rees@divenz.co.nz
Dive Shop: no **Rentals:** yes
Air: yes **Courses:** yes
Boat: *Pacific Hideaway* (15m, 25 divers)
Trips: Poor Knights Islands

Paihia Dive
50 Williams Road, Paihia
☎ 09-402 7551 fax: 09-402 7110
toll-free ☎ 0800-107 551
www.divenz.com
divepaihia@xtra.co.nz
Dive Shop: yes **Rentals:** yes
Air: yes **Courses:** yes
Boats: *Pacific Star* (12m, 14 divers), *Deep Six*
(8.5m, 10 divers)
Trips: *Rainbow Warrior*, Bay of Islands

The Dive Connection
140 Lower Cameron St., Whangarei
☎ 09-430 0818 fax: 09-430 0562
diveconn@ihug.co.nz
Dive Shop: yes **Rentals:** yes
Air: yes **Courses:** yes

Tutukaka Charters
Tutukaka Marina, Tutukaka
☎ 09-434 3818 fax: 09-434 3755
www.sportfishing.co.nz/diving.htm
fish@clear.net.nz
Other: Booking agent for Tutukaka dive boats

Whangaroa Harbour Motor Camp
320 Whangaroa Harbour Road
☎/fax: 09-405 0306
www.whangaroa.tripod.com
dyleewhangaroa@xtra.co.nz
Dive Shop: yes **Rentals:** yes
Air: yes **Courses:** no
Boat: *Dylee* (6m, 4 divers)
Trips: *Rainbow Warrior*, Cavalli Islands

Hauraki Gulf & Auckland

Adventure Education Training
12G Puhinui Road, Manukau City
☎ 09-277 6888 fax: 09-277 7712
toll-free ☎ 0800-386 236
www.adventureeducation.co.nz
aetmanukau@xtra.co.nz
Dive Shop: yes **Rentals:** yes
Air: yes **Courses:** yes

Cascade Dive Scuba Services
141 Cascades Road, Pakuranga
☎ 09-576 4634 fax: 09-576 2764
Dive Shop: yes **Rentals:** yes
Air: yes **Courses:** yes
Boat: *Dive Inn* (5.7m, 4 divers)
Trips: Hauraki Gulf

Dive Centre Limited
128 Wairau Road, Takapuna, Auckland
☎ 09-444 7698 fax: 09-444 6948
toll-free ☎ 0800-863 483
www.divecentre.co.nz
dive.centre.ltd@xtra.co.nz
Dive Shop: yes **Rentals:** yes
Air: yes; nitrox available **Courses:** yes
Boat: *Divercity* (14m, 16 divers)
Trips: Hauraki Gulf

Dive HQ Greenlane
135 Greenlane Road, Greenlane
☎ 09-520 7300 fax: 09-520 7302
www.divehq.co.nz
info@divehqgreenlane.co.nz
Dive Shop: yes **Rentals:** yes
Air: yes; nitrox available **Courses:** yes

Dive HQ Hibiscus Coast
673 Whangaparaoa Road, Whangaparaoa
☎ 09-424 8513 fax: 09-424 8540
toll-free ☎ 0800-102 102
www.divehq.co.nz
coastdive@hotmail.com
Dive Shop: yes **Rentals:** yes
Air: yes **Courses:** yes
Boats: *Scubee 1* (5m, 6 divers), *Scubee 2* (6m, 8 divers)
Trips: Hauraki Gulf

Dive HQ Northshore
121G Rosedale Road, Albany
☎ 09-478 3418 fax: 09-478 3418
toll-free ☎ 0800-102 102
www.divehq.co.nz
info@divehqnorthshore.co.nz
Dive Shop: yes **Rentals:** yes
Air: yes **Courses:** yes

Dive HQ West Auckland
5 Portage Road, New Lynn
☎ 09-827 7008 fax: 09-826 1566
toll-free ☎ 0800-102 102
www.divehq.co.nz
info@divehqwest.co.nz
Dive Shop: yes **Rentals:** yes
Air: yes; nitrox available **Courses:** yes

Dive Venture New Zealand
3 Gibraltar Crescent, Parnell
☎ 09-302 2191 fax: 09-358 2221
www.diveventure.co.nz

cheli@xtra.co.nz
Dive Shop: yes **Rentals:** yes
Air: no **Courses:** yes

Dolphin Explorer
Pier 3, Quay Street, Auckland
☎ 09-357 6032 fax: 09-357 6035
www.dolphinexplorer.com
aucklanddolphins@xtra.co.nz

Fergs Fish & Dive Spot
The Marina, Half Moon Bay
☎ 09-534 9083 fax: 09-537 3942
Dive Shop: yes **Rentals:** yes
Air: yes **Courses:** yes

Goat Island Dive
142A Pakiri Road, Leigh
☎ 09-422 6925 fax: 09-422 6926
toll-free ☎ 0800-348 369
www.goatislanddive.co.nz
dive@goatislanddive.co.nz
Dive Shop: yes **Rentals:** yes
Air: yes **Courses:** yes
Boat: *Te Tohora* (7.8m, 12 divers)
Trips: Hauraki Gulf

Goat Island Scuba Safaris
21 Hauraki Road, Leigh
☎ 09-422 6708 fax: 09-422 6709
http://geocities.com/divingnewzealand
goatislandscuba@hotmail.com
Dive Shop: yes **Rentals:** yes
Air: yes **Courses:** yes
Boat: *Scuba Diver* (8m, 9 divers)
Trips: Hauraki Gulf, Northland

North Shore Scuba Centre
5/20 Constellation Drive, Mairangi Bay
☎ 09-478 6220 fax: 09-478 9995
www.divecompressors.co.nz
airtec@ihug.co.nz
Dive Shop: yes **Rentals:** yes
Air: yes **Courses:** no

Orakei Dive Shop
234 Orakei Road, Remuera
☎ 09-524 2117 ☎/fax: 09-524 6268
www.orakeidive.co.nz
joanne@orakeidive.co.nz
Dive Shop: yes **Rentals:** yes
Air: yes **Courses:** yes

Orewa Water Sports
22 Hillary Square, Orewa
☎ 09-426 8283 fax: 09-426 8288
Dive Shop: no **Rentals:** no
Air: yes **Courses:** no

Performance Diver (NZ)
72 Barrys Point Road, Takapuna
☎ 09-489 7782 fax: 09-489 7783
www.performance-diver.co.nz
sales@performance-diver.co.nz
Dive Shop: yes **Rentals:** yes
Air: yes **Courses:** yes

Hauraki Gulf & Auckland (continued)

Port Fitzroy Dive Station
Fitzroy Wharf, Great Barrier Island
☎ 09-429 0591
divebottle@xtra.co.nz
Dive Shop: yes **Rentals:** yes
Air: yes **Courses:** no

Scubamania NZ
17 Glen Road, Browns Bay
☎ 09-478 3359 fax: 09-476 3528
www.freedomdive.co.nz
freedomdive@xtra.co.nz
Dive Shop: yes **Rentals:** yes
Air: yes; nitrox available **Courses:** yes

**Seafriends Marine Conservation &
Education Centre**
7 Goat Island Road, Leigh
☎ 09-422 6212 fax: 09-422 6245
www.seafriends.org.nz
sea.friends@xtra.co.nz
Dive Shop: no **Rentals:** yes
Air: yes **Courses:** no

Snells Beach Dive & Fishing
Mahurangi Shopping Centre, Snells Beach
☎ 09-425 5324 fax: 09-425 5324
Dive Shop: yes **Rentals:** yes
Air: yes **Courses:** no

Stirlings Specialist Dive Shop
349 Dominion Road, Mount Eden
☎ 09-630 0178 fax: 09-631 5900
www.stirlingsdive.co.nz
neil@stirlingsdive.co.nz
Dive Shop: yes **Rentals:** yes
Air: yes **Courses:** yes

The Dive Doctor
106 Potts Road, Whitford
☎/fax: 09-530 8117
dis.divedoc@xtra.co.nz
Other: Equipment service, repair and sales

The Scuba Experience
3 Trugood Place, East Tamaki
☎ 09-272 2284 fax: 09-272 2242
john@puc.co.nz
Dive Shop: yes **Rentals:** yes
Air: yes; nitrox available **Courses:** yes
Boats: 5m, 4 divers; 6m, 6 divers
Trips: Hauraki Gulf

Warkworth Boat & Fishing Centre
22 Whitaker Road, Warkworth
☎ 09-425 8490 fax: 09-425 0032
www.fishingthegulf.co.nz
boatnfish@xtra.co.nz
Dive Shop: no **Rentals:** no
Air: yes **Courses:** no

Coromandel Peninsula

Academy Divers International
24-27 Albert Road, Mackaytown, Paeroa
☎ 07-862 8959 fax: 07-862 7444
toll-free ☎ 0800-112 131
www.academydivers.co.nz
a.d.i@wave.co.nz
Dive Shop: no **Rentals:** yes
Air: yes **Courses:** yes

Cathedral Cove Dive & Snorkel
2 Grange Court, Hahei Beach
☎ 07-866 3955 fax: 07-866 3053
www.hahei.co.nz
ccdive@hahei.co.nz
Dive Shop: yes **Rentals:** yes
Air: yes **Courses:** yes
Boat: *Mekong Rose* (6m, 6 divers)
Trips: Cathedral Cove to Hot Water Beach

Coromandel Fish & Dive Centre
95 Kapanga Road, Coromandel
☎ 07-866 8797 fax: 07-866 7257
Dive Shop: yes **Rentals:** yes
Air: yes **Courses:** yes

Tairua Dive & Fishinn
The Esplanade, Paku Boat Ramp, Tairua
☎/fax: 07-864 8054
tairuadiveandfishinn@xtra.co.nz
Dive Shop: yes **Rentals:** yes
Air: yes **Courses:** yes
Boat: 8m, 8 divers
Trips: Aldermen Islands, Coromandel coast

Whangamata Sports & Marine
607C Port Road, Whangamata
☎ 07-865 9300 fax: 07-865 9700
Dive Shop: no **Rentals:** yes
Air: yes **Courses:** no

Bay of Plenty

Action Dive Rotorua
26 Depot St., Rotorua
☎ 07-350 2303 fax: 07-350 2304
toll-free ☎ 0800-386 236
actiondive@clear.net.nz
Dive Shop: yes **Rentals:** yes
Air: yes **Courses:** yes

Adventure Education Training
154 1st Ave. W., Tauranga
☎ 07-571 4350 fax: 07-571 4360
toll-free ☎ 0800-386 236
www.adventureeduction.co.nz
info@adventureeducation.co.nz
Dive Shop: yes **Rentals:** yes
Air: yes **Courses:** yes
Boat: *Adventurekoru* (16.2m, 40 divers)
Trips: Bay of Plenty

Bay of Plenty (continued)

Dive HQ Tauranga
213 Cameron Road, Tauranga
☎/fax: 07-578 4050
toll-free ☎ 0800-102 102
info@diveshop.co.nz
Dive Shop: yes **Rentals:** yes
Air: yes; nitrox available **Courses:** yes
Boat: *Marco* (13m, 10 divers)
Trips: Bay of Plenty

Dolphins Down Under
2 The Strand, Whakatane
☎ 07-308 4636 fax: 07-308 0359
toll-free ☎ 0800-354 7737
www.dolphinswim.co.nz
dolphinswim@dolphinswim.co.nz

Dolphin Seafaris
90 Maunganui Road
Mount Maunganui
☎ 07-575 4620
toll-free ☎ 0800-326 8747
www.nzdolphin.com
bookings@nzdolphin.com

John's Dive Shop
1122 Eruera St., Rotorua
☎ 07-348 0750 fax: 07-349 6128
johnsdive@xtra.co.nz
Dive Shop: yes **Rentals:** yes
Air: yes **Courses:** yes

Kawerau MWG Mitre 10
10 Liverpool St., Kawerau
☎ 07-323 7779 fax: 07-323 6247
Dive Shop: no **Rentals:** tanks only
Air: yes **Courses:** no

Mount Dive Shop
21 Newton St., Mount Maunganui
☎/fax: 07-575 4418
Dive Shop: yes **Rentals:** yes
Air: yes **Courses:** no

Reel 'n' Wave
29 Wilson Road, Waihi Beach
☎ 07-863 5859 fax: 07-863 5539
Dive Shop: no **Rentals:** yes
Air: yes **Courses:** no

Tauranga Underwater Centre
50 Cross Road, Sulphur Point, Tauranga
☎ 07-571 5286 fax: 07-571 5287
www.diveunderwater.com
colindue@xtra.co.nz
Dive Shop: yes **Rentals:** yes
Air: yes; nitrox available **Courses:** yes
Boat: *Pacific Runner* (6m, 8 divers)
Trips: Bay of Plenty

The Tauranga Dolphin Co.
194 16th Ave., Tauranga
☎ 07-578 3197
toll-free ☎ 0800-836 574
www.swimwithdolphins.co.nz
taurangadolphins@clear.net.nz

Whakatane SportsWorld
186 The Strand, Whakatane
☎ 07-307 0714 fax: 07-307 0765
toll-free ☎ 0800-348 394
www.divewhite.co.nz
sportsworldwhk@xtra.co.nz
Dive Shop: yes **Rentals:** yes
Air: yes **Courses:** yes
Boat: *Black Shag* (9m, 8 divers)
Trips: White Island, Bay of Plenty

Central North Island

Adventure Education Training
4/24 Norton Road, Hamilton
☎ 07-847 2220 fax: 07-847 2720
toll-free ☎ 0800-386 236
www.adventureeducation.co.nz
aethamilton@xtra.co.nz
Dive Shop: yes **Rentals:** yes
Air: yes **Courses:** yes

Club Scuba
University of Waikato
Gate 1, Knighton Road, Hamilton
☎ 07-834 3954 fax: 07-834 3953
www.clubscuba.co.nz
dive@clubscuba.co.nz
Dive Shop: yes **Rentals:** yes
Air: yes **Courses:** yes

Dive HQ Hamilton
401 Anglesey St., Hamilton
☎ 07-834 1435 fax: 07-838 3869
toll-free ☎ 0800-102 102
www.divehq.co.nz
team@divehqhamilton.co.nz
Dive Shop: yes **Rentals:** yes
Air: yes; nitrox available **Courses:** yes

Dive HQ Palmerston North
552-554 Main St., Palmerston North
☎ 06-358 6911 fax: 06-357 2281
toll-free ☎ 0800-427 375
www.divehq.co.nz
ldsports@xtra.co.nz
Dive Shop: yes **Rentals:** yes
Air: yes **Courses:** yes

Divers Supplies
437 Queen St., Masterton
☎/fax: 06-378 6492
www.diversupplies.co.nz
diver@contact.net.nz
Dive Shop: yes **Rentals:** yes
Air: yes **Courses:** yes
Boat: 6m, 6 divers
Trips: Castlepoint

Dive Shack
26 Spa Road, Taupo
☎/fax: 07-378 1926
Dive Shop: yes **Rentals:** yes
Air: yes **Courses:** yes

Central North Island (continued)

Manawatu Dive & Marine Centre
664 Tremaine Ave., Palmerston North
☎ 06-355 1464 fax: 06-355 1465
toll-free ☎ 0800-272 822
manawatu.dive@xtra.co.nz
Dive Shop: yes **Rentals:** yes
Air: yes **Courses:** yes
Boat: 6m, 6 divers
Trips: Kapiti Coast

Scuba Scene Taupo
42 Tamamutu St., Taupo
☎ 07-376 8014 fax: 07-376 8015
toll-free ☎ 0800-728 227
www.scubascene.co.nz
info@scubascene.co.nz
Dive Shop: yes **Rentals:** yes
Air: yes **Courses:** yes

Waikato Dive Centre
451 Te Rapa Road, Hamilton
☎ 07-849 1922 fax: 07-849 1942
toll-free ☎ 0800-434 846
www.waikatodive.co.nz
waikato.dive@xtra.co.nz
Dive Shop: yes **Rentals:** yes
Air: yes; nitrox available **Courses:** yes

Wanganui Underwater Dive Centre
447 Victoria St., Wanganui
☎ 06-348 7747 fax: 06-343 3303
commdives@xtra.co.nz
Dive Shop: yes **Rentals:** yes
Air: yes **Courses:** yes
Boat: *Ocean Spirit* (8.2m, 10 divers)
Trips: Kapiti Coast, Mana, Marlborough Sounds

East Coast

Adventure Dive
118 Taradale Road, Napier
☎ 06-843 5148 fax: 06-843 5149
toll-free ☎ 0800-386 236
www.adventuredive.co.nz
info@fun2do.co.nz
Dive Shop: yes **Rentals:** yes
Air: yes; nitrox available **Courses:** yes

Adventure Education East Cape
359 Gladstone Road, Gisborne
☎ 06-868 4588 fax: 06-868 5222
toll-free ☎ 0800-868 458
www.adventuredive.co.nz
david@fun2do.co.nz
Dive Shop: yes **Rentals:** yes
Air: yes **Courses:** yes

Dive HQ Gisborne
308 Gladstone Road, Gisborne
☎ 06-868 6686 fax: 06-867 8102
toll-free ☎ 0800-102 102
www.divehq.co.nz
spgis@clear.net.nz

Dive Shop: yes **Rentals:** yes
Air: yes **Courses:** yes

Dive HQ Hastings
709 Karamu Road, Hastings
☎ 06-878 8831 fax: 06-878 7810
www.divehq.co.nz
Dive Shop: yes **Rentals:** yes
Air: yes **Courses:** yes

Dive HQ Napier
Nelson Quay, Ahuriri, Napier
☎ 06-834 2009 fax: 06-834 2019
www.divehq.co.nz
divehqnapier@xtra.co.nz
Dive Shop: yes **Rentals:** yes
Air: yes **Courses:** yes

Wainui Dive
28 Wairere Road, Wainui Beach, Gisborne
☎ 06-867 9450 fax: 06-867 9450
wainuidive@xtra.co.nz
Dive Shop: yes **Rentals:** yes
Air: yes **Courses:** yes

Taranaki

Blue Line Dive
151 St. Aubyn St., New Plymouth
☎ 06-758 3100 fax: 06-757 4422
rhinestonz@clear.net.nz
Dive Shop: yes **Rentals:** yes
Air: yes **Courses:** yes
Boat: *The Classroom* (5.4m, 6 divers)
Trips: Sugar Loaf Islands

New Plymouth Underwater
16 Hobson St., New Plymouth
☎ 06-758 3348 fax: 06-759 4996
www.newplymouthunderwater.co.nz
info@newplymouthunderwater.co.nz

Dive Shop: yes **Rentals:** yes
Air: yes; nitrox available **Courses:** yes
Boat: *Sportscat XI* (7.3m, 10 divers)
Trips: Sugar Loaf Islands

Ron Opie Diving
329 Garsed Road, Patea
☎/fax: 06-273 4271
toll-free ☎ 0800-674 334
ron.opie@xtra.co.nz
Dive Shop: yes **Rentals:** yes
Air: yes **Courses:** yes
Boat: *Yellowfin* (6m, 7 divers)
Trips: Patea coast

Wellington

Dive & Ski
14 Waione, Petone
☎ 04-568 5028 fax: 04-568 4560
toll-free ☎ 0800-288 288
www.diveski.co.nz
diveski@clear.net.nz
Dive Shop: yes **Rentals:** yes
Air: yes; nitrox available **Courses:** yes

Divers World
57 Rugby St., Wellington
☎ 04-385 8533 fax: 04-385 8349
toll-free ☎ 0800-348 347
www.diversworld.co.nz
diversworld.wgtn@xtra.co.nz
Dive Shop: yes **Rentals:** yes
Air: yes **Courses:** yes

Dive Spot
9 Marina View, Mana, Wellington
☎ 04-233 8238 fax: 04-233 9580
toll-free ☎ 0800-348 323
www.divespot.co.nz
thedivespot@xtra.co.nz
Dive Shop: yes **Rentals:** yes
Air: yes **Courses:** yes
Boat: *Mana Diver* (6.5m, 8 divers)
Trips: Wellington, Mana, Kapiti

Island Bay Divers
353 The Parade, Island Bay
☎ 04-383 6778 fax: 04-383 6073
www.ibdivers.co.nz
tim@ibdivers.co.nz

Dive Shop: yes **Rentals:** yes
Air: yes **Courses:** yes
Boat: *Prion* (6m, 8 divers)
Trips: Wellington, Kapiti

Kapiti Dive Centre
27 Milne Drive, Paraparaumu
☎ 04-298 9554 fax: 04-298 7546
www.southernocean.co.nz
southernocean@xtra.co.nz
Dive Shop: yes **Rentals:** yes
Air: yes **Courses:** yes

NZ Sea Adventures
17B Hartham Place, Porirua
☎ 04-237 8989 fax: 04-236 8747
www.scubadiving.co.nz
tony@scubadiving.com
Dive Shop: yes **Rentals:** yes
Air: yes; nitrox available **Courses:** yes
Boat: *Kahu* (6m, 8 divers)
Trips: Wellington coast, Kapiti, Mana

Splash Gordon
432 The Esplanade, Island Bay
☎ 04-939 3483 fax: 04-939 8101
www.splashgordon.co.nz
dive@splashgordon.co.nz
Dive Shop: yes **Rentals:** yes
Air: yes; nitrox available **Courses:** yes
Boat: *Waverunner* (6m, 6 divers)
Trips: Wellington south coast

Marlborough

Abel Tasman Seal Swim
Main Road, Riwaka, Motueka
☎ 03-527 8136
☎ 0800-527 8136
www.nelson.net.nz//web/sealswim
sealswim@xtra.co.nz

Big Blue Dive & Fish
1 Akersten St., Port Nelson
☎ 03-546 7411 fax: 03-546 7422
www.bigbluenz.com
bigblue@ts.co.nz
Dive Shop: yes **Rentals:** yes
Air: yes **Courses:** yes
Boat: *Big Blue 2* (5.2m, 5 divers)
Trips: Marlborough Sounds, Tasman Bay

Blenheim Dive Centre
9 Scott St., Blenheim
☎ 03-578 0331 fax: 03-577 6066
bdc@xtra.co.nz
Dive Shop: yes **Rentals:** yes
Air: yes **Courses:** yes
Boat: *BDC2* (6m, 6 divers)
Trips: Marlborough Sounds

**Diverse Divers International/
Motueka Underwater**
466 High St., Motueka
☎/fax: 03-528 4680
www.diversedivers.co.nz

ed@diversedivers.co.nz
Dive Shop: yes **Rentals:** yes
Air: yes; nitrox available **Courses:** yes
Boat: *KDS1* (6m, 5 divers)
Trips: Marlborough Sounds

Divers World
corner of London Quay & Auckland St.
Picton
☎ 03-573 7323 fax: 03-573 8876
www.pictondiversworld.co.nz
pictondiversworld@xtra.co.nz
Dive Shop: yes **Rentals:** yes
Air: yes **Courses:** yes

Motueka SportsWorld
201 High St., Motueka
☎ 03-528 9845 fax: 03-528 9446
www.sportsworld.co.nz
sportsworldmot@xtra.co.nz
Dive Shop: yes **Rentals:** yes
Air: yes **Courses:** no

Richmond SportsWorld
213 Queen St., Richmond, Nelson
☎ 03-544 8290 fax: 03-544 1765
www.sportsworld.co.nz
sportsworld.richmond@xtra.co.nz
Dive Shop: yes **Rentals:** yes
Air: yes **Courses:** yes

Marlborough (continued)

Sandpiper Charters
59 Broadway, Picton
☎ 03-573 8882 fax: 03-573 8885
www.sandpiper.co.nz
frankcarre@xtra.co.nz

Dive Shop: no **Rentals:** yes
Air: yes; nitrox available **Courses:** no
Boat: *Sandpiper* (13m; 12 divers daytrips, 6
divers live-aboard)
Trips: Marlborough Sounds, Fiordland

Canterbury

Dive HQ Christchurch
70 Moorhouse Ave., Christchurch
☎ 03-379 5804 fax: 03-379 5808
0800-102 102
www.diveskiworld.com
divehq@diveskiworld.com
Dive Shop: yes **Rentals:** yes
Air: yes **Courses:** yes
Boat: *DiveHQ* (5.8m, 8 divers)
Trips: Akaroa, Kaikoura, Motanau

Dive Werks
351 Port Hills Road, Christchurch
☎/fax: 03-332 7445
www.divewerks.co.nz
sales@divewerks.co.nz
Dive Shop: yes **Rentals:** yes
Air: yes **Courses:** yes

Dolphin Encounter, Kaikoura
58 West End, Kaikoura
☎ 03-319 6777 fax: 03-319 6534
toll-free ☎ 0800-733 365
www.dolphin.co.nz
info@dolphin.co.nz

Dolphin Experience, Akaroa
61 Beach Road, Akaroa
☎/fax: 03-304 7726
toll-free ☎ 0508-365 744
www.dolphinsakaroa.co.nz
dolphin.experience@xtra.co.nz

Kaiapoi Dive Shop
187A Ohoka Road, Kaiapoi
☎ 03-327 7777 fax: 03-327 9111
Dive Shop: yes **Rentals:** yes
Air: yes **Courses:** yes
Boat: 6m, 5 divers
Trips: Motunau, Kaikoura, Akaroa

Moby Dick's Dive Centre
35 Moorhouse Ave., Christchurch
☎ 03-377 6260 fax: 03-377 6261
mobydicks@clear.net.nz
Dive Shop: yes **Rentals:** yes
Air: yes **Courses:** yes

New Zealand Sea Adventures
94 West End, Kaikoura
☎ 03-319 6622 fax: 03-319 6868
toll-free ☎ 0800-728 223
www.scubadive.co.nz
nzsa.wildlife@xtra.co.nz
Dive Shop: yes **Rentals:** yes
Air: yes **Courses:** yes
Boat: *Seaquest* (6.5m, 10 divers)
Trips: Kaikoura
Other: Seal swimming

Seal Swim Kaikoura
202 Esplanade, Kaikoura
☎ 03 319 6182
www.kaikoura.co.nz/sealswim
sealswim@clear.net.nz

Shark Dive Kaikoura
25 Beach Road, Kaikoura
☎ 03-319 6888 fax: 03-319 5713
toll-free ☎ 0800-225 297
www.sharkdive.co.nz
sharkdive@ihug.co.nz

Topspot Kaikoura Backpackers & Sealswims
22 Deal St., Kaikoura
☎ 03-319 5540 fax: 03-319 6587
topspot@xtra.co.nz

Underwater Sports
431 Tuam St., Christchurch
☎ 03-389 5353 fax: 03-389 5364
toll-free ☎ 0800-386 236
www.adventureeducation.co.nz
rwebster@clear.net.nz
Dive Shop: yes **Rentals:** yes
Air: yes **Courses:** yes

Whyte Scuba Diving
9 Alexandra St., Timaru
☎ 03-688 6860 fax: 03-688 1110
toll-free ☎ 0800-322 929
whytehotmail@xtra.co.nz
Dive Shop: yes **Rentals:** yes
Air: yes **Courses:** yes

Otago

Dive Otago
2 Wharf St., Dunedin
☎ 03-466 4370 fax: 03-466 4371
www.diveotago.co.nz
info@diveotago.co.nz
Dive Shop: yes **Rentals:** yes
Air: yes **Courses:** yes

Boats: *Sea Squirt* (5.8m, 9 divers), *Sea Slug*
(4.2m, 5 divers)
Trips: Otago, Fiordland, Stewart Island

Wilsons Sports Centre
223 Thames St., Oamaru
☎ 03-434 8231 fax: 03-434 7973
Dive Shop: yes **Rentals:** yes
Air: yes **Courses:** yes

Southland, Fiordland & Stewart Island

Dive HQ Invercargill/Outdoor World
27 Tay St., Invercargill
☎ 03-214 2052 fax: 03-214 2041
toll-free ☎ 0800-102 102
www.divehq.co.nz
divehqinvercargill@hjsmith.co.nz
Dive Shop: yes **Rentals:** yes
Air: yes **Courses:** yes

Dive HQ Queenstown
c/o Element, Remarkables Park, Frankton
☎ 03-442 2445 fax: 03-442 2446
divehq@elementnz.com
Dive Shop: yes **Rentals:** yes
Air: yes **Courses:** yes

Dolphin Magic, Waikawa
611 Waikawa–Niagara Road
☎/fax: 03-246 8444
toll-free ☎ 0800-377 581
dolphinmagic@xtra.co.nz

Fiordland Ecology Holidays
5 Waiau St., Manapouri
☎ fax: 03-249 6600
toll-free ☎ 0800-249 660
www.fiordland.gen.nz
eco@xtra.co.nz
Dive Shop: no **Rentals:** yes
Air: yes **Courses:** no
Boat: *Breaksea Girl*, (20m, 10 divers)
Trips: Fiordland, Stewart Island

Southern Aqua Adventures
100 Gore St., Bluff
☎ 03-212 7757 fax: 03-212 7737
southern.aqua@xtra.co.nz
Dive Shop: yes **Rentals:** yes
Air: yes **Courses:** yes
Boat: *Kiri Waipai* (11m, 13 divers)
Trips: Foveaux Strait, Stewart Island

Stewart Island Dive Centre
Main Road, Oban, Stewart Island
☎/fax: 03-219 1456
Dive Shop: yes **Rentals:** yes
Air: yes **Courses:** no

Takaroa 2 Adventure Cruises
233 Barrow St., Bluff
☎/fax: 03-212 8170
takaroa@ihug.co.nz
Dive Shop: no **Rentals:** tanks & weight belts
Air: yes **Courses:** no
Boat: *Takaroa 2* (17m, 12 divers)
Trips: Stewart Island, Fiordland

Talisker Charters
11 View St., Stewart Island
☎/fax: 03-219 1151
www.taliskercharter.co.nz
tait@taliskercharter.co.nz
Dive Shop: no **Rentals:** no
Air: yes **Courses:** no
Boat: *Talisker* (17m, 6 divers)
Trips: Stewart Island, Fiordland

Tawaki Dive
44 Caswell Road, Te Anau
☎ 03-249 9006
www.tawakidive.co.nz
sarahdave@tawakidive.co.nz
Dive Shop: yes **Rentals:** yes
Air: yes **Courses:** yes
Boat: *Tawaki* (6m, 5 divers)
Trips: Milford Sound

Westland Diver Services
32 Ballance St., Runanga, Greymouth
☎ 03-762 7465 fax: 03-762 7462
westland_diver_services@xtra.co.nz
Dive Shop: yes **Rentals:** yes
Air: yes **Courses:** yes

Diving Resources

AquaAdventure NZ
47 Kauri Point Road, Laingholm, Auckland
☎ 09-816 9386 fax: 09-816 9478
www.aquaadventure-nz.com
aquaadventurenz@aol.com
Other: Travel agency specializing in NZ diving tours; German-speaking

Dive New Zealand/Dive Pacific
P.O. Box 55-069, Mission Bay, Auckland
☎ 09-521 0684 fax: 09-521 3675
www.divenewzealand.com
divenz@divenewzealand.co.nz
Other: Bimonthly diving magazine, diving book distributor

New Zealand Underwater Association
1/40 Mount Eden Road, Auckland
☎ 09-623 3252 fax: 09-623 3523
www.nzunderwater.org.nz

nzu@nzunderwater.org.nz
Other: Publish bimonthly diving magazine, environmentally active

Northland Underwater Photographic Club
c/o R. Armstrong
60 Motel Road, Tutukaka
☎ 09-434 3290

Oceans Society of New Zealand
P.O. Box 26-007, Epsom, Auckland
www.oceanz.org
info@oceanz.org

Royal New Zealand Navy Hydrographic Business Unit
19 Byron St., Takapuna, Auckland
toll-free ☎ 0800-628 924
www.navyhydro.co.nz
sales@hydrographic.co.nz

Diving Resources (continued)

Underwater Photographic Society of New Zealand
c/o W. Curry
29 Edgeworth Road
Glenfield, Auckland
☎ 09-444 1070

Wellington Underwater Photographic Club
c/o J. Long
35 Monaghan Ave., Karori
☎ 04-476 9638

Visitor Information Centres

Akaroa Information Centre
☎ 03-304 8600
www.akaroa.com
akaroa.info@clear.net.nz

Bay of Islands Information Centre
☎ 09-402 7345 09-402 7314
visitorinfo@fndc.govt.nz

Blenheim Visitor Information Centre
☎ 03-578 9904
blm_info@clear.net.nz

Christchurch & Canterbury Visitor Information Centre
☎ 03-379 9629 fax: 03-377 2424
www.christchurchnz.net
info@christchurchnz.net

Dunedin Visitor Centre
☎ 03-474 3894 fax: 03-474 3311
www.cityofdunedin.com
visitor.centre@dcc.govt.nz

Fiordland Travel Visitor Centre
☎ 0800-656 501
www.fiordlandtravel.co.nz
info@fiordlandtravel.co.nz

Gisborne Visitor Information Centre
☎ 06-868 6139 fax: 06-868 6138
www.gisbornenz.com
info@gisbornenz.com

Hokianga Information
☎ 09-405 8869 fax: 09-405 8317
fndchka@xtra.co.nz

Information Far North
☎ 09-408 0879 fax: 09-408 2546
fndckta@xtra.co.nz

Kaikoura Visitor Information Centre
☎ 03-319 5641
www.kaikoura.co.nz
info@kaikoura.co.nz

Marlborough Information & Travel Centre
☎ 03-577 8080 fax: 03-577 8079
www.destinationmarlborough.com
mvic@destinationmarlborough.com

Napier Visitor Information Centre
☎ 06-834 1911 fax: 06-835 7219
www.hawkesbaynz.com
info@napiervic.co.nz

Nelson Visitor Information Centre
☎ 03-548 2304
www.nelsonnz.com
vin@nelsonnz.com

New Plymouth District Information Centre
☎ 06-759 6080
www.newplymouthnz.com
info@newplymouth.govt.nz

New Zealand Tourism
03-379 4886
www.tourism.net.nz
enquiries@tourism.net.nz

Picton Visitor Information Centre
☎ 03-573 7477 fax: 03-573 5021
www.destinationmarlborough.com
pictonvin@xtra.co.nz

Stewart Island Visitor Information Centre
☎ 03-219 1218 fax: 03-219 1555
www.stewartisland.co.nz
stewartislandfc@doc.govt.nz

Tairua Information Centre
☎ 07-864 7575
www.thecoromandel.com/informationcentre.html
info.tairua@xtra.co.nz

Tauranga Information & Visitors Centre
☎ 07-578 8103
www.gotauranga.co.nz/visinfo.htm
info@visitplenty.co.nz

Tourism Auckland Centre
☎ 09-979 7070 fax: 09-979 7080
www.aucklandnz.com
citysails@aucklandnz.com

Warkworth Information Centre
☎ 09-425 9081
www.warkworth-information.co.nz
service@warkworth-information.co.nz

Wellington Visitor Information Centre
☎ 04-802 4860 fax: 04-802 4863
www.wellingtonnz.com
info@wellingtonnz.com

Whakatane Visitor Information Centre
☎ 07-308 6058 fax: 07-308 6020
www.whakatane.com
whakataneinfo@xtra.co.nz

Whitianga Information Centre
☎ 07-866 5555
www.visitor.net.nz
enquiries@visitor.net.nz

Index

dive sites covered in this book appear in **bold** type

Lonely Planet Pisces Books

The **Diving & Snorkeling** guides cover top destinations worldwide. Beautifully illustrated with full-color photos throughout, the series explores the best diving and snorkeling areas and prepares divers for what to expect when they get there. Each site is described in detail, with information on suggested ability levels, depth, visibility and, of course, marine life. There's basic topside information as well for each destination.

Also check out dive guides to:

Australia: Southeast Coast	Cayman Islands	Honduras' Bay Islands	Seychelles
Bahamas	Cocos Island	Jamaica	Southern California & the Channel Islands
Baja California	Cozumel	Maldives	
Belize	Cuba	Monterey Peninsula & Northern California	Texas
Bermuda	Curaçao		Trinidad & Tobago
Bonaire	Dominica	Pacific Northwest	Turks & Caicos
British Virgin Islands	Guam & Yap	Puerto Rico	Vanuatu
		Scotland	